"In books like *The Myth of a Ch[ristian Nation]* Greg Boyd has proven to be one o[f ...] on the planet. Now, with *God Lo[oks Like Jesus]*  with M. Scott Boren and written a simple but profound reflection on Jesus. 'Jesus is the answer' might sound too rudimentary, but the truth is this: Jesus is the best critique of what has gone wrong in Christianity. In a day when all kinds of racism and bigotry and nationalism and prosperity and violence are trying to camouflage themselves as Christianity, Boyd and Boren remind us all: the word Christian means 'Christlike.' If it doesn't look like Jesus, and love like Jesus, and show compassion like Jesus—it is not of God. Because God is and always has been like Jesus. And we are called to follow. God, give us the courage."

—SHANE CLAIBORNE, author, activist, and cofounder of Red Letter Christians

"Greg Boyd works to counter the 'good cop/bad cop' caricature that some people have of God (even if unconsciously), where Jesus in the New Testament is pitted against Israel's God in the Old Testament (with the Holy Spirit as a vague bystander). Boyd invites us to re-examine our perceptions of God without ignoring the Old Testament depictions of divinely sanctioned violence that were to be carried out by ancient Israel. *God Looks Like Jesus* is an accessible yet challenging book that implores us to employ our theological imaginations."

—DENNIS R. EDWARDS, dean and vice president for church relations at North Park Theological Seminary and the author of *Humility Illuminated: The Biblical Path Back to Christian Character*

"It is no secret that the 'Christian' brand repeatedly finds ways to drift from the Jesus way into toxic images of God and a gospel distorted by the idols and ideologies of our age. In *God Looks Like Jesus*, Boyd and Boren recenter our theology and practice in a way that is wondrously (even scandalously) 'Jesus-y.' They demonstrate how a Christ-centered theology that transcends sloganeering leads to real-life liberation on the ground. This book offers the church and beyond a much needed spiritual bath!"

—BRADLEY JERSAK, president of St. Stephen's University and author of the More Christlike trilogy

"I have deep respect for pastors and leaders like Greg Boyd who are willing to wrestle with theological constructs at the deepest level and be transformed by what they discover. In *God Looks Like Jesus*, Boyd writes with humility, wisdom, and lived experience that challenges our faith and calls us to practice following Jesus more fully, more freely, more expansively."

—**KATHY ESCOBAR**, cofounder of The Refuge and author of *Faith Shift: Finding Your Way Forward When Everything You Believe Is Coming Apart* and *Practicing: Changing Yourself to Change the World*

"Jesus is God with a face. I can't tell you who first said that, but I have long believed it to be true. In *God Looks Like Jesus*, Boyd and Boren demonstrate how this simple truth has revolutionary implications. When we truly grasp that Jesus—not our philosophical constructs or religious traditions—reveals God's character, everything changes. This book isn't just a theological treatise; it is an invitation to fall in love with a God who looks more like a crucified savior than a celestial dictator."

—**JONATHAN MERRITT**, columnist and author of *Learning to Speak God from Scratch: Why Sacred Words Are Vanishing—and How We Can Revive Them*

"The strength of this book lies in its simplicity. In a world that often mistakes God's power for human might, Boyd and Boren reveal a radical truth: Jesus' self-giving love is the fullest picture of God. With theological depth and pastoral warmth, this book will inspire, unsettle, and draw readers deeper into the beauty of a Jesus-centered faith."

—**JEREMY DUNCAN**, author of *Upside-Down Apocalypse: Grounding Revelation in the Gospel of Peace*

"In this short, accessible, and yet remarkably informative book, Boyd and Boren help us (re)discover the good news of a God who looks like Jesus. I loved reading *God Looks Like Jesus*, and as a pastor I am even more excited to give this book away to others and to have it as a resource to learn and encounter the love of God revealed in Christ. This is the exactly the kind of book I've been waiting for!"

—**JONNY MORRISON**, pastor and author of *Prodigal Gospel: Getting Lost and Found Again in the Good News*

God Looks Like Jesus

God Looks Like Jesus

A Renewed Approach to Understanding God

Gregory A. Boyd
with **M. Scott Boren**

Harrisonburg, Virginia

Herald Press
PO Box 866, Harrisonburg, Virginia 22803
www.HeraldPress.com

Produced in partnership with

Study guides are available for many Herald Press titles at www.HeraldPress.com.

GOD LOOKS LIKE JESUS
© 2025 by Herald Press, Harrisonburg, Virginia 22803. 800-245-7894.
  All rights reserved.
Library of Congress Control Number: 2025935622
International Standard Book Number: 978-1-5138-1551-0 (paperback);
  978-1-5138-1552-7 (ebook)
Printed in United States of America
Design by Merrill Miller

All rights reserved. This publication may not be reproduced, stored in a retrieval system, or transmitted in whole or in part, in any form, by any means, electronic, mechanical, photocopying, recording or otherwise without prior permission of the copyright owners.

All scripture quotations, unless otherwise indicated, are taken from the Holy Bible, New International Version®, NIV®. Copyright © 1973, 1978, 1984, 2011 by Biblica, Inc.® Used by permission of Zondervan. All rights reserved worldwide. www.zondervan.com The "NIV" and "New International Version" are trademarks registered in the United States Patent and Trademark Office by Biblica, Inc.® Scripture quotations marked (KJV) are taken from the King James Version. Scripture quotations marked (NRSVue) are from New Revised Standard Version Bible, Updated Edition. Copyright © 2021, National Council of Churches of Christ in the United States of America. Used by permission. All rights reserved worldwide. Scriptures marked (ISV) are taken from the Holy Bible: International Standard Version©. Dopyright © 1996–2012 by The ISV Foundation. All rights reserved internationally. Used by permission.

29 28 27 26 25   10 9 8 7 6 5 4 3 2 1

Contents

Foreword 9
Introduction 13

1   The One Eternal Word 19
2   The Center of the Center 33
3   Cross-Tinted Glasses 51
4   Literary Crucifixes 65
5   The Jesus-Looking Kingdom. 89
6   Rethinking God 105
7   The Blessed Hope 117

Appendix: My Approach to Scripture 129
Acknowledgments 131
Notes 133
The Authors 143

Foreword

"Don't all Christians think that God looks like Jesus?"

This question invariably follows every time I mention that I'm part of a global movement seeking to recenter Jesus in Christian faith and practice.

It's a reasonable thing to ask. After all, churches vary wildly in everything from worship style to political passions. But you can generally count on finding a cross somewhere in the building. You can expect Jesus' name to be invoked in songs and prayers and calls to action. The assumption of Jesus' unique role seems baked into the title "Christ-ian."

Yet surface similarities in symbol and language can obscure a deeper truth: all Christians do not, in fact, believe that God looks like Jesus—at least, not in the complete, encompassing way that Greg Boyd describes in this book. Images of God and God's character and ideas about God's intent and desires are shaped by a variety of forces. Family dynamics, cultural values, religious trauma, political ideology, personal proclivities, and the interpretative lens we bring to the Bible can all influence, and often distort, our vision of the face of God.

Even those who call themselves followers of Jesus often carry mental pictures of God and God's desires that are "Jesus, and . . ." or "Jesus, but . . ." Our impressions and ideas aren't yet fully conformed to the extraordinary discovery at the heart of biblical revelation: "Jesus, period." Jesus, in whom the fullness of God was pleased to dwell (Colossians 1:19). Jesus, who is God's Word enfleshed (John 1:14). Jesus, whose defining representation surpasses every other (Hebrews 1:1–3). Jesus, in whom we see the Father (John 14:9). Jesus, the corrective lens to all ideology, interpretation, and intuition.

For most of my life, I thought I believed in a God who looks like Jesus. Only recently have I begun to discover how much of the image of God I carry is out of alignment with Jesus. The Spirit has drawn me onto a journey in which many of my deepest instincts are being disciplined by the stories of Jesus and healed by encounter with him. A simple question is changing my life: What if I believed that God really is who Jesus says?

Like Boyd, I am convinced that our picture of God is the key to radically faithful living. If we come to believe that God is as near, as gracious and forgiving, as reliably generous as Jesus claims, everything changes. We are freed to take great risks, to make new sacrifices and alternative investments, to practice indiscriminate love that defies polarization. Discovering a God like Jesus doesn't lower the moral bar but raises it exponentially, transforming our whole humanity.

To many people it seems like Christianity, at least in the West, is hitting a dead end. It is not the end that many predicted—one brought on by the rise of science and the sense that faith can no longer be rationally justified. In fact, mysticism and spiritual curiosity appear to be on the rise. The dead end stopping Christianity in its tracks in the twenty-first century turns out to be a problem of character: portraits of God that are ugly and violent and all too frequently mirrored in the actions of God's living worshipers.

But there is a better Christian story, proclaimed by the church from the very start. The story of God definitively revealed to the world in Jesus, who described himself as "gentle and humble" (Matthew 11:29) and overcame evil with the unexpected power of self-giving love. The story of a people who are being transformed by God's Spirit into that same image and deployed into the world with that same power of cross-shaped healing and disruption.

Greg Boyd has had the audacity to write a book making the case for the most obvious truth in Christian faith—which, it turns, has not been so obvious at all. The story he tells of how this truth has transformed his life is far from unique to him. Rather, Greg is one voice in a growing movement of individuals and churches who are finding their lives turned inside out by the revolutionary discovery that God really does look like Jesus, always has, and always will.

Greg and I find ourselves closely connected these days through a community called Jesus Collective, which is working together to amplify and equip a movement grounded on this core rediscovery. We celebrate and serve this global movement. But no organization or leader owns it. We believe what we are witnessing in our time is an organic movement of the Spirit, working to draw the church around Jesus again.

Despite all the rumors to the contrary, there is hope. There is hope for the world. There is hope for the church. There is hope for you. And that hope is rooted where it has always been—in a Jesus-looking God, who loves the world with relentless devotion, and in a Jesus-looking people, who will love it with him, for his sake.

—Meghan Larissa Good, author of
*Divine Gravity: Sparking a Movement
to Recover a Better Christian Story*

Introduction

*It behooves us to be careful what we worship,
for what we are worshiping we are becoming.*
—ATTRIBUTED TO **RALPH WALDO EMERSON**

I became a Christian at seventeen in an austere, sectarian Pentecostal church. While there was much that was not healthy in this church, I remain deeply grateful for that chapter in my life. By nature, I lean toward extremes, and the more mainstream expressions of Christianity I had encountered before failed to stir me. But this church? It was serious! So serious that I quit the rock band I drummed for, discarded the drugs I was using, stopped going to concerts, movies, or sporting events, and even gave away my beloved collection of rock albums. (I was told to burn them, but I couldn't bring myself to do it.) All the above was considered sinful.

Giving up these worldly attachments was surprisingly easy. What clung to me like an iron shackle, however, was my bondage to pornography. Today, unfortunately, such material is as accessible to young people as the air we breathe, but in the mid-1970s, when I became a Christian, access required a peculiar blend of circumstance and "luck." After my father and my stepmother divorced when I was thirteen, my father—an atheist with strong convictions about social justice but a baffling moral blind spot regarding sex—made no effort to conceal his sizable cache of pornography. And so, for four years prior to my conversion, I became enslaved to an addiction.

I had hoped that my bondage would be broken when I surrendered to Christ. I was told that "the power of the Holy Ghost will set you free from sin," but it didn't happen. What made matters much worse was that, according to the theology of this church, every single sin severed one's salvation until repentance mended the rift. As a result, I spent my early Christian walk feeling like a yo-yo on God's salvation finger, getting "saved" and "unsaved" on a weekly, and sometimes daily, basis.

Two years into this exhausting spiritual charade, I snapped. Guilt and frustration had curdled into something darker: an angry resignation. I had tirelessly pleaded with God to break the chains of my addiction, but the heavens seemed as silent as stone. On a brisk October night in 1976, I decided to give up the fight.

I typically would get "re-saved" at our Sunday evening church service, which always ended with an altar call to repentance. At the close of this night's service, however, I could not bring myself to go forward. What was the point? I knew I'd fall back into sin in a day or two. When the church service had ended, I stood in the emptying church parking lot with a friend, the one person to whom I had confessed my secret struggle. He too had ready access to his dad's porn, though he still clung to the hope of being set free. I honestly felt like I was doomed to eternal hell and there was nothing I could do about it. I was in the darkest pit of despair I could imagine.

As we talked beside his battered truck, however, my despair morphed into rage. The parking lot now empty, my voice rose into a crescendo of anger and obscenity. The truth came out: I despised this meticulously legalistic, perpetually disappointed God I'd been futilely striving to please. I exploded in a tirade against God that shocked even me. I hurled accusations, blasphemies, and venomous rage, shouting into the indifferent night sky. What did I have to lose?

I recall my friend backing away from me a couple steps at the height of my outburst, presumably to be out of harm's way when God smote me for my diabolic insolence.

I wasn't conscious of this at the time, but now I realize I wasn't just railing against my inability to meet God's holy standards. I was unloading a lifetime of pent-up fury at every authority I had angered and disappointed—which was pretty much every authority in my life. The nuns and priests at the Catholic elementary school who were exasperated by my ADHD-fueled antics. My stepmother, whose cruel punishments taught me that love was conditional and fragile and could turn cruel at the drop of a dime. And now, God himself—a divine tyrant who, I believed, had set me up to fail by infusing me with hormones I couldn't control and putting me in a home with unlimited access to porn. All so he could delight in watching me flounder before casting me into eternal fire.

My rage eventually burned itself out, and I sank into silent despair. My friend eventually broke the silence. "We must be missing something," he whispered. "Why can other people 'live the life' when we can't?"

His question irritated me. I flung my King James Bible onto the hood of his truck while shouting, "I've read this book cover to cover, so if we're missing something, where the hell is it?" I looked down at my Bible, which had flopped open. I sarcastically read the first verse my eyes happened upon. It was Romans 8:1. "There is therefore now no condemnation to them which are in Christ Jesus?" I sneered. "Is that supposed to be our magical solution?"

Something about the verse snagged my attention. I read it again, more slowly, less sarcastically, and then again. Something shifted. I'd read this passage before, but it suddenly felt shockingly new. "There is therefore now no condemnation . . ." My voice faltered. I turned to my friend who was more confused about what was taking place than I was. "What does that even mean?" I asked, my sarcasm giving way to genuine curiosity.

I slowly read the verse once again and then proceeded through the rest of the chapter, and as I did, something within began to come alive.

> What shall we then say to these things? If God be for us, who can be against us? . . .
> Who shall lay anything to the charge of God's elect? It is God that justifieth. (Romans 8:31–33 KJV)

I didn't understand all that Paul was saying, but for the first time, I began to get a glimpse of a beautiful God whose love was not contingent upon my good behavior. A God who did not measure my worth by my ability to meet God's standards but who embraced me as I was—broken, flawed, and yet unimaginably beloved.

That night, the veil lifted. The God I had always imagined—a harsh taskmaster, a celestial accountant tallying my sins—was replaced by a vision of a God who loved me with an unrelenting, sacrificial love. The unbearable weight of doom lifted off my shoulders and was replaced by joy, and tears, and laughter, and an enormous sense of relief.

For the first time in my life, I realized that God, the ultimate authority, was not like all the other authority figures in my life whom I had always disappointed and angered. God loved and accepted me for free, and this changed everything.

For the first time, I felt a desire to find freedom from my porn addiction that was anchored in love, not fear. And love,

I have since learned, is a much greater motivator for bringing about change than fear could ever be. There would still be occasional struggles, but the six-year stronghold that porn had had on me was finally broken.

My experience on that pivotal evening, followed by years of reflection, has convinced me that the way we envision God is the single most important thing in our life. Our mental picture of God determines the depth of our love for God and the extent to which that love transforms our attitude and actions. Our love for God and the passion with which we live our life for Christ will never surpass the lovability of our mental image of God.

The apostle Paul underscores this idea in 2 Corinthians. He observes that unbelievers have a "veil" over their minds (2 Corinthians 3:13–14). "But whenever anyone turns to the Lord," he says, "the veil is taken away" (v. 16). Then Paul waxes eloquent. "Now the Lord is the Spirit, and where the Spirit of the Lord is, there is freedom. And we all, who with unveiled faces contemplate the Lord's glory, are being transformed into his image with ever-increasing glory, which comes from the Lord, who is the Spirit" (vv. 17–18).

Where the Spirit of the Lord is at work, there is freedom—freedom to envision something in our minds that we were previously prevented from seeing. And what we are now empowered to behold with our "unveiled faces" is the "Lord's glory," or, as Paul states it several verses later, we can see "the light of the knowledge of God's glory displayed in the face of Christ" (4:6).

Most importantly, as we "contemplate" this glory, we are "transformed into his image with ever-increasing glory." For Paul, growing in Christlikeness is not a matter of merely putting forth your best effort. We are rather transformed into the beauty of Christ when the Spirit opens our spiritual eyes to envision the beauty of God shining through Jesus Christ.

This is what first began to happen to me in my church's parking lot on that brisk October night back in 1976. And it's why I claim that our mental image of God is the most important thing in our life.[1] If our conception of God is veiled or distorted, as mine was, it can't help but stifle our love for God and hinder our spiritual transformation. But when we learn to imaginatively behold the true God who is fully revealed in Jesus Christ, we are liberated to grow into the fullness of life God intends for us. In the end, this is the heart of the gospel: to see God rightly, to know God deeply, and to reflect God faithfully.

The purpose of this short book is to help readers form a clearer and more beautiful mental picture of God by demonstrating that God looks like Jesus and exploring how this profound truth transforms our theology and, more importantly, our lives.

It is my prayer that the Spirit will use this book to open the spiritual eyes of readers, enabling them to behold the glorious love of God shining in the face of Jesus Christ and to be transformed into his image "with ever-increasing glory."[2]

1

The One Eternal Word

Jesus is what the Father has to say to us.
—**C. S. LEWIS**, *MERE CHRISTIANITY*

In 2015, the Reverend Gay Byrne interviewed Dr. Stephen Fry, a renowned atheist, on the Irish television program called *The Meaning of Life*. At one point Byrne asked Fry what he would say to "the Almighty" should he encounter God after death. Every word of Fry's response cut like a blade, honed by a smoldering indignation that could hardly be contained.

"I'll say: 'Bone cancer in children? What's that about? How dare you? How dare you create a world in which there is such misery that is not our fault? It's not right. It's utterly, utterly evil! Why should I respect a capricious, mean-minded, stupid God who creates a world that is so full of injustice and pain?' That's what I would say."[1]

Fry doesn't believe in God, but he's clearly enraged by the mental conception of the God he rejects—a capricious deity who is directly responsible for all the suffering and injustice we see in the world.

If I thought that this is what "God" is like, I'd feel morally obliged to join Fry in his rebellion. Fortunately, the God I believe in looks nothing remotely like the God whom Fry understandably rejects. For the God I believe in looks like Jesus, and Jesus is altogether beautiful.

The ambiguity of "God"

We tend to assume that everyone means the same thing when they talk about God. We don't. The word "God" is shrouded in ambiguity, conjuring up radically different images in people's minds.

For some, such as Stephen Fry, the word "God" evokes visions of a stern, vengeful judge, meting out retribution in the form of plagues or disasters. For others, it evokes a micromanaging deity, predestining every detail—including the damnation of souls. Some envision a God so remote and dispassionate that he's virtually irrelevant, while others imagine God as a nebulous, impersonal force vibrating through the universe. Some picture God as a doting grandpa who just wants his grandkids to have fun. Others—advocates of the "classical view" of God—imagine him existing in a timeless eternal moment, unaffected by anything outside himself.

No one, of course, has a fully accurate conception of God, if for no other reason than the fact that God transcends everything our finite minds can think or imagine. How, for example, can you imagine a being who never began and has no bounds? You can't.

But is there at least a way to assess whether someone's image of God points in the right direction?

At this point, many Christians instinctively appeal to the Bible—and they have good reason to. Based on the way Jesus treated the Old Testament and preauthorized the writing of the New Testament, Christians have always revered the Bible as the inspired story of God.[2] I share this conviction.

The question, however, is how we should approach the Bible, for the approach you take to Scripture completely determines the "God" you find in it. Many Christians, for example, assume that believing in the inspiration of the Bible means they must consider each and every one of its differing depictions of God to be equally accurate and authoritative. The result is a conception of God who has a loving and merciful side, revealed in Christ, but who also has an ominous violent side, capable of commanding the extermination of entire populations, to give just one example (e.g., Deuteronomy 7:1–2).[3]

I contend that the New Testament does not assume all biblical depictions of God carry equal authority. Instead, it considers Jesus to be the sole, perfect revelation of God's character and purposes for the world.

The radiance of God's glory

To begin, the author of Hebrews captures the supremacy of the revelation of God in Christ when he writes: "In the past God spoke to our ancestors through the prophets at many times and in various ways, but in these last days he has spoken to us by his Son, whom he appointed heir of all things, and through whom also he made the universe. The Son is the radiance of God's glory and the exact representation of his being, sustaining all things by his powerful word" (Hebrews 1:1–3).

As is true of the New Testament as a whole, this author ascribes full divinity to the Son.[4] He claims that, while God spoke through prophets in the past, in these last days—this final epoch of history—God has spoken to us *in person*.

Moreover, the Son is "the radiance of God's glory." The Greek term translated "radiance" (*apaugasma*) refers to something that shines forth from a source, like light from the sun. The term translated "glory" (*doxa*) is associated with the visible splendor and majesty of God. This author is thus claiming that the Son is the light God emits whenever he displays the splendor and majesty of his being. And in doing this, the Son reveals God down to his very essence (*hypostasis*). There is no part of God that the Son does not reveal.

As theologian Michael Ramsey puts it: "God is Christlike, and in him there is no un-Christlikeness at all."[5] There is no shadow side to God, no hidden un-Christlike dimension to his being. Whenever God shines, and whenever God speaks, it looks like Jesus. This is why Jesus must be the filter through which we assess all conceptions of God—especially our own.

The New Testament resounds with this same Christocentric emphasis. One of the clearest expressions comes from Paul's letter to the Colossians, where he emphatically states: "For in Christ all the fullness of the Deity lives in bodily form" (Colossians 2:9).

Paul presents Jesus not as a mere reflection or fragment of God, but as the living, breathing embodiment of the entire divine essence. He confronts the influence of Gnostics, who imagined God's fullness (*pleroma*) was diffused across a hierarchy of angels. They argued that knowing God's *pleroma* required traversing this hierarchy, accumulating secret revelations of the divine *pleroma* along the way. Christians, they claimed, limited themselves by tethering their understanding of God to Jesus alone.[6] They roughly parallel people immersed in New Age thinking today, in which Jesus is typically looked up to as an "enlightened teacher" who reveals an aspect of God, but who also look to other "enlightened teachers" or books to reveal other aspects of God.

There is of course nothing wrong with gleaning wisdom from wherever or whomever wisdom is to be found. But when it comes to revealing the truth of God's character and purposes for the world, Paul's response to the Gnostics is a clarion call: the *pleroma* of God isn't scattered across angelic orders or an assortment of enlightened teachers—it is fully and perfectly found in Christ.

Paul emphasizes this with unrelenting clarity:

"All" (*pan*)—not just some.

"Fullness" (*pleroma*)—not just a part.

"Of the Deity" (*theotes*)—not some lesser spiritual entity.

Paul couldn't be more emphatic. He claims that everything that makes God *God* was fully embodied in Jesus.

To the degree that we trust Christ as the full revelation of God's character, there can be no suspicion that there might be aspects of God's fullness that we might glean from other sources, angelic or otherwise.

The One who reveals the Father

John powerfully reinforces this truth. He opens his gospel by declaring: "In the beginning was the Word, and the Word was with God, and the Word was God" (John 1:1).

Note the definite article. God doesn't have many words; God has one. This "Word" is both "with God" and is himself "God." The Word is God facing outward, as it were, revealing himself to the world. Insofar as anyone's image or depiction of God discloses the truth about God, it is this one eternal Word, Jesus Christ, whom they are encountering. In the words of Hans Urs von Balthasar, "The central Word which God speaks and which comprises, as their unity and end, all the manifold words of God, is Jesus Christ, the incarnate God. . . . His life is the fulfilling of Scripture."[7]

Similarly, Scott Swain notes that, while God speaks in a wide diversity of ways throughout the progress of revelation, "ultimately God speaks *the same* Word . . . the word Christ."[8]

John goes on to declare: "The Word became flesh and made his dwelling among us. We have seen his glory, the glory of the one and only Son, who came from the Father, full of grace and truth" (John 1:14). John is claiming that Jesus is what the glorious God looks like when the facing-outward dimension of God's being takes the form of a human being. Through this human, Jesus Christ, we can behold God's glory.

A little later, John notes: "For the law was given through Moses; grace and truth came through Jesus Christ. No one has ever seen God, but the one and only Son, who is himself God and is in closest relationship with the Father, has made him known" (John 1:17–18).

John uses sight as a double entendre, signifying both physical sight and intellectual understanding, as in, "I see your point."[9] John thus claims that no one ever physically saw God, and no one really understood God, until the Word became flesh. As great as the law of Moses was, we only understood the truth about God's grace when Jesus revealed it.

This theology of the Word permeates John's gospel. For example, in chapter 14, Jesus was teaching about God the Father when Philip suddenly asked him, "Lord, show us the Father and that will be enough for us." Jesus' response was shocking: "Anyone who has seen me has seen the Father. How can you say, 'Show us the Father'?" (John 14:9). If you want to know what the Father is like, Jesus claimed, don't look anywhere other than to him. He alone is the way to the Father, the truth of the Father, and the life of the Father (John 14:6).

In sum, the New Testament does not present Jesus as part of what God is like or as one revelation of God among others. Jesus reveals the truth about God's character down to God's very essence. All other depictions of God in Scripture—and all the ways we imagine God in our minds—must be assessed by this singular revelation.

A weightier authority

A powerful indicator of Jesus' incomparable authority in revealing God is that Jesus places his authority over that of the Old Testament. For example, Jesus said to the Pharisees, "I have testimony weightier than that of John" (John 5:36). What is interesting is that Jesus elsewhere told people, "Truly I tell you, among those born of women there has not risen anyone greater than John the Baptist; yet whoever is least in the kingdom of heaven is greater than he" (Matthew 11:11).

So, John is the greatest prophet leading up to Jesus, which would include all Old Testament prophets, and yet Jesus claims he has a testimony that is "weightier" than John's. The clear implication is that Jesus' authority supersedes that of any Old Testament author.

One of the clearest expressions of the superior authority of Jesus is that, while he certainly shared his Jewish contemporaries' view that all Scripture is divinely inspired, he also was nevertheless not afraid of repudiating it when he felt led by his Father to do so. While conservative exegetes have made valiant attempts to avoid this conclusion, it is hard to deny that Jesus taught things that "blatantly contradict and overturn multiple Old Testament passages and principles," as Derek Flood observes.[10]

For example, while the Old Testament commands—not merely allows—people to make oaths in God's name (Deuteronomy 6:13), Jesus forbade it (Matthew 5:33–36). In fact, curiously enough, he added that anything beyond a simple "'Yes' or 'No' . . . comes from the evil one" (Matthew 5:37). Similarly, while the law stressed the importance of distinguishing between "clean" and "unclean" animals (Leviticus 11), Jesus taught that "nothing outside a person can defile them by going into them. Rather, it is what comes out of a person that defiles them" (Mark 7:15; compare Acts 10:15; Romans 14:3; 1 Corinthians 10:31).

So, too, when Jesus was touched by a woman "who had been subject to bleeding for twelve years" (Luke 8:43), he did not rebuke her, even though the law stipulated that women with this sort of disorder were "unclean" and that anyone who touched them, or even touched anything they had touched, needed to purify themselves by washing themselves and their clothes (Leviticus 15:25–27).

The woman trembled in fear once it was discovered what she had done, undoubtedly anticipating a harsh response from Jesus (Luke 8:47). But Jesus instead addressed her with a term of endearment, calling her "daughter." In doing so, he affirmed her purity-defying act as an act of faith that healed her (v. 48). Moreover, it is not without significance that Jesus did not remove himself from the crowd to purify himself once this episode was over, as the law required.

What is for our purposes the most important example of Jesus placing his authority over the Old Testament concerns its "eye for eye" and "tooth for tooth" commands (Exodus 21:23–24; Leviticus 24:19–20; Deuteronomy 19:21), often referred to as the lex talionis, or "law of just retribution." In stark contrast to this law, Jesus instructed people to "not resist an evil person," adding that "if anyone slaps you on the right cheek, turn to them the other cheek also" (Matthew 5:38–39).

In this light, Kenton Sparks is hardly overstating the matter when he acknowledges that Jesus "freely admitted that his ethical teachings contrasted sharply with some of the ethical teachings in the Mosaic law."[11] Eugene Boring offers an insightful word when he notes that this "juxtaposition is not to be softened," for in repudiating the lex talionis and replacing it with his own teachings about loving enemies (Matthew 5:44–45), "Jesus does more than give a better interpretation of the old authority; he relocates authority from the written text of Scripture to himself—i.e., to God's presence in his life, teaching, death, and resurrection."[12]

It seems apparent that by replacing the lex talionis with his instruction to "not resist an evil person," to "turn the other cheek," and to "love your enemies," Jesus was calling on people to respond to wrongdoers in a way that is "the direct opposite" of the commandments in the Old Testament, as Flood notes.[13]

Jesus clearly did not consider his testimony to be merely on a par with the testimony of the Old Testament, as though everything in Scripture carried equal weight. He rather considered his testimony to be weightier.

The divinity and humanity of Jesus

The assertion that Jesus is both God and human stands as one of the most profound paradoxes of Christian theology. The New Testament leaves no room for doubt concerning Jesus' full humanity. Jesus experienced human limitations. He had to grow in wisdom (Luke 2:52) and learn obedience through suffering, just like the rest of us (Hebrews 5:8). He felt hunger, fatigue, sorrow, and the full range of human emotions. He was tempted in every way we are, though he lived a sinless life (Hebrews 4:15). And, of course, as a human being, Jesus could be murdered, as he was on the cross.

Yet, alongside these affirmations of his humanity, the New Testament unmistakably declares Jesus to be fully God. Beyond the verses already addressed, we see this in Thomas's confession as he finally beholds the resurrected Christ and exclaims, "My Lord and my God!" (John 20:28). And note, Jesus not only accepted Thomas's acclamation, he commends his faith (v. 29).

Moreover, in his first epistle, John refers to Jesus as "the true God and eternal life" (1 John 5:20), and in Paul's letters, we find Jesus referred to as "God over all" (Romans 9:5) and "our great God and Savior" (Titus 2:13).

These aren't isolated incidents. The New Testament brims with divine ascriptions to Jesus.[14] The most common title given to Jesus is "Lord" (*kurios*), a term synonymous with Yahweh, the sacred name of God in the Hebrew Scriptures (e.g., Acts 16:31; Romans 4:24; 1 Corinthians 15:57; Galatians 6:14). He is portrayed as Judge and Creator—roles every Jew knew were reserved for God alone (Matthew 25:31–46; Colossians 1:15–19). Even more strikingly, in Revelation, Jesus identifies himself as "the Alpha and the Omega" (Revelation 22:13), a title spoken by God in the same book (Revelation 1:8) and claimed by Yahweh in Isaiah (Isaiah 41:4; 44:6; 48:12).

One of the most startling revelations of Jesus' divinity occurs when he declares, "Before Abraham was born, I am" (John 8:58). The peculiar grammar is no accident—Jesus is deliberately identifying himself with Yahweh, the great I AM who spoke to Moses from the burning bush (Exodus 3:14). His audience grasped his meaning immediately, as evidenced by their attempt to stone him for blasphemy.

Equally compelling is how Jesus is treated in matters of worship and prayer. Scripture is unequivocal: only God is to be worshiped and prayed to. Yet throughout the New Testament, we see Jesus being addressed in prayer and worshiped (e.g., 1 Corinthians 1:2; 2 Corinthians 12:8). What makes this especially striking is that this exaltation of Jesus arose among first-century monotheistic Jews who vehemently opposed the pagan practice of divinizing humans. That such a group would ascribe divine status to Jesus underscores how extraordinary their experience of him must have been.

The weight of evidence led the early church to the conclusion expressed at the Council of Chalcedon in 451 CE: Jesus Christ is both "fully God and fully human." While this creed set the boundaries for orthodox belief about Jesus, it didn't resolve the paradox of how divinity and humanity coexist fully in him.

Two Christological models

How should we understand the relationship between Jesus' divine and human natures? Many theologians in the Christian tradition have proposed a "two minds" Christology.[15] This view suggests that Jesus simultaneously possessed both the all-knowing mind of God and the finite mind of a human. According to this perspective, Jesus experienced life both as a human subject and as God, pointing to moments when he seemed omniscient—such as discerning people's hidden thoughts (Matthew 9:4; John 2:24–25) or foreseeing future events (Luke 22:31–34; John 13:18–27).

However, as traditional as this approach is, it presents significant difficulties. It requires us to imagine Jesus as simultaneously aware of every molecule in the cosmos while also being an unaware infant in Mary's arms. To me, this seems less like a legitimate paradox and more like a blatant contradiction, akin to describing a "married bachelor" or a "round square." It claims that Jesus was simultaneously omniscient and not omniscient—a contradiction that, in my view, cannot be resolved.

An alternative understanding, known as "kenotic Christology," offers a way to affirm Jesus' full divinity and humanity while avoiding this apparent contradiction.[16] This model is rooted in Philippians 2, where Paul describes how the Son of God "emptied himself" (*kenosis*) to become fully human (Philippians 2:7 NRSVUE). According to this view, Christ willingly relinquished the exercise of certain divine attributes—such as omniscience, omnipresence, and omnipotence—precisely so he could live as a true human being, with all the limitations that entails.

Within this framework, when Jesus demonstrated supernatural knowledge or power, it wasn't because he was inherently omniscient or omnipotent. As Jesus himself explained, he depended entirely on the Father to reveal knowledge to him and on the Spirit to supernaturally empower him (e.g., Matthew 12:28; John 5:19, 30).

In my opinion, this model is not only more coherent than the traditional two minds Christology; it also has profound implications for discipleship. If Jesus retained unrestricted access to his divine attributes, aspiring to follow his example would be futile. But if Jesus lived fully as a human, relying on the Father and the Spirit, then his life becomes a pattern we can emulate—an invitation to live in total dependence on God.

If Jesus set aside the exercise of divine omnipotence, omniscience, and omnipresence to become human, what did he retain that qualifies him to be God? For advocates of a kenotic Christology, the New Testament provides the answer: "God is love" (1 John 4:8). And John defines the kind of love God is by pointing us to the cross: "This is how we know what love is: Jesus Christ laid down his life for us" (1 John 3:16).

The kind of love that God eternally is was fully embodied in Jesus throughout his life and ministry. But, as I'll discuss in the following chapter, it was most perfectly displayed when Jesus laid down his life to redeem us and all creation. This is why Jesus in the gospel of John refers repeatedly to the crucifixion as "the hour" for which he was sent into the world (John 2:4; 7:30; 8:20; 12:23, 27; 13:1; 16:32; 17:1).

When Hebrews declares that the Son is "the exact representation of [God's] being" (Hebrews 1:3), it is the other-oriented love of God's eternal essence that he is referring to. Jesus is exactly what the eternal love of God looks like when fully imprinted on a human being. This is what I mean when I say, "God looks like Jesus."

Our relationship with God is always mediated through our mental picture of God, which is why paying attention to the various ways you imagine God is so vitally important. It is also why deciding who you're going to trust to base your mental picture of God on is so important. Considering the material covered in this chapter, our image of God shouldn't be based on our subjective intuitions or our own reasoning. Nor should it be based merely on what our parents, pastors, or teachers have told us. Indeed, while all Scripture is divinely inspired, our image of God shouldn't even be based on Old Testament portrayals of God to the degree that these portrayals conflict with Jesus' revelation of God, as I'll discuss in chapter 3.

Our image of God should rather be anchored in Jesus Christ, the one and only Word of God, the one and only revelation of God, the one and only Person who has made the otherwise unknown God known (John 1:17–18). For Jesus alone is the exact representation of God, down to his very essence.

God looks like Jesus. But this forces the question, which Jesus? People interpret the life and ministry of Jesus in rather different ways. To this question we now turn.

2

The Center of the Center

God is never more fully God ... than in the powerlessness and humiliation of the cross. Far from contradicting the divine omnipotence, the cross supremely reveals it. Nothing demonstrates more fully than the cross how great is the omnipotence of God's love.

—GEORGE HUNSINGER, *DISRUPTIVE GRACE*

Over the last century, beginning with Karl Barth, an increasing number of theologians, exegetes, and preachers have claimed to be "Christocentric" in their theologizing and interpretation of Scripture. What is curious, however, is that these Christocentric theologians, exegetes, and preachers often arrive at very different interpretations of Scripture as well as different views of God. How is this possible?

One primary reason is that biblical and theological scholars emphasize different aspects of Jesus' life, depending upon the picture of God that they bring with them. For example, some highlight the cleansing of the temple (John 2:13–17) and Jesus' command to the disciples to purchase swords on the night of his arrest (Luke 22:35–38) to argue that "Jesus wasn't entirely opposed to the use of force when circumstances demanded it."[1] On these grounds they claim that "Jesus, as Yahweh incarnate, upholds the moral perfection of God's commands, including those involving judgment and war."[2]

It's a bit of a stretch, if you ask me. In the temple incident, John says Jesus made a makeshift whip to drive out the animals (John 2:15). He simply cracked the whip, which is still a common way of startling animals to quickly steer them in a certain direction. There is no indication that any animals, let alone people, were harmed. And while it's true Jesus told his disciples to purchase swords, it wasn't because he intended for them to use them. Look what happened when Peter tried (John 18:10–11). Jesus rather explains that the swords were necessary for him to be "numbered with the transgressors" (Luke 22:37). In other words, Jesus needed to give the temple guards plausible grounds for having him arrested as an insurrectionist.

In my estimation, events like this could only be used to support an image of God commanding violence if this was the preconception of God that scholars brought to their reading of the Gospels. And it's not hard to understand why, because the Old Testament narrative sometimes depicts God along these lines. But rather than starting with Jesus and then looking for a way to reinterpret the Scriptures' violent portraits of God in this light (as I will propose in chapters 3 and 4), these scholars start with the violent portraits and then interpret Jesus' teachings and actions in this light.

In the previous chapter I made the case that Jesus is the center of Scripture. In what follows, I will contend that there is a center to this center, for everything Jesus was about culminates in his crucifixion.[3] As such, I contend that the cross should serve as the interpretive lens through which we understand Jesus' life and ministry as well as the whole of Scripture.

The choice to prioritize Jesus' crucifixion over everything else is not based on a subjective whim. Rather, it is rooted in the New Testament itself.

The love that God eternally is

Christians have always professed that "God is love"(1 John 4:8). Unfortunately, the word "love," like the word "God," can mean different things to different people. The Christians who carried out the Crusades and the Inquisition and slaughtered alleged heretics and witches professed that "God is love." The many Christians who believe that multitudes of people were predestined by God to go to eternal hell also profess that "God is love," though some admit it is a difficult doctrine.[4]

So, what do we mean when we say that God is love? The question could not be more important because your mental conception of God could not be more important. Fortunately, the New Testament answers this question in a clear and decisive way. "This is how we know what love is: Jesus Christ laid down his life for us. And we ought to lay down our lives for our brothers and sisters" (1 John 3:16).

To know what love is—the kind of *agape* love that God eternally is—we must not look to our fallen intuition, experience, or reason. We must rather keep our eyes firmly fixed on the cross.

≈≈≈

Cross-like, or cruciform, love is the throughline of Jesus' entire ministry. While Jesus' teaching that we see the Father when we see Jesus (John 14:9) was true at every moment of his life, the character of the Father is most unambiguously disclosed when Jesus allowed himself to be crucified. The cross culminates, expresses, and weaves together everything Jesus was about—namely, revealing the true, enemy-embracing, nonviolent, self-sacrificial, loving character of his Father.

In my view, a truly Christocentric approach to understanding God and interpreting Scripture requires an approach that centers the cross. If correct, it means we should not interpret what Jesus was about through the lens of the temple incident or Jesus' command to buy swords or any other particular teaching or action. We should rather interpret everything Jesus was about, everything God is about, and everything Scripture is about through the lens of the crucifixion. In short, we should consider the "crucified Christ" to be "the key for all the divine secrets of Christian theology," in the words of German theologian Jürgen Moltmann.[5]

And the reason we should view the cross in this fashion is because this is the way the New Testament frames it.

The cross in the synoptic gospels

The first indication of the centrality of the cross in the New Testament is the fact that all the synoptic gospels are structured around their "passion narratives," which refer to each of their accounts of Jesus' suffering and death. One famous New Testament scholar went so far as to say, "One could call the Gospels passion narratives with extended introductions."[6] The narrative of the synoptic gospels points forward to, and climaxes in, the revelation of Jesus on the cross.

Second, the centrality of the cross in the Gospels is reflected in the fact that each of the synoptic gospels depicts Jesus trying to break through his disciple's preconceived notions about the Messiah by teaching them that he had to go to Jerusalem to "suffer many things" and to be executed (Matthew 16:21; 17:23; 20:19; 26:2; Mark 10:32–34; Luke 17:25; 24:7).

Third, the way Jesus redefined power points to a cross-centered understanding. Jesus repeatedly stated that he had not come into the world to "be served, but to serve, and to give his life as a ransom for many" (Matthew 20:28; Mark

10:45). This and many similar teachings anticipate the kind of humble, weak-appearing power revealed on the cross.

Fourth, Jesus taught his disciples, "Love your enemies and pray for those who persecute you, that you may be children of your Father in heaven. He causes his sun to rise on the evil and the good, and sends rain on the righteous and the unrighteous" (Matthew 5:44–45).

We are to love our enemies and to pray for those who persecute us *so that* we "may be children of [the] Father in heaven." This is the benchmark Jesus sets for us. For it is only when we love like this that we reflect the way our Father loves—indiscriminately, like the rain falls and the sun shines (Matthew 5:45; Luke 6:34–35). This indiscriminate love finds its quintessential expression on the cross, as Jesus offers up his life, and prays for the forgiveness of the very people who were crucifying him (Luke 23:34).

Fifth, the centrality of the cross in the synoptic gospels is reflected in the fact that many of the most surprising aspects of the cross are anticipated throughout Jesus' ministry. For example, few people in Jesus' day would have expected God to "justify" a tax collector who was too ashamed to "even look up to heaven" (Luke 18:10–14) instead of the righteous Pharisee who fasted twice a week, gave a tenth of all he earned to God, and who thanked God he was not like "robbers, evildoers, adulterers" or "this tax collector" (vv. 11–12). Similarly, no first century Jew expected God to welcome into his kingdom "tax collectors and prostitutes" before religious leaders whom everyone held in high esteem (Matthew 21:31; compare Luke 7:38–50).

Indeed, because the God whom Jesus revealed was so contrary to what people expected, Jesus announced repeatedly that those whom most assumed were outsiders would find themselves inside, while those whom most assumed were insiders would find themselves out (e.g., Matthew 7:21–23; 22:1–9; 25:31–46). All of these aspects of Jesus' ministry anticipate the great reversal of the cross, where God entered into total solidarity with outsiders and sinners.

Jesus also astounded, and confounded, the religious establishment by his countercultural behavior. Jesus broke long-established and often biblically based social taboos when it was loving to do so. He served, interacted with, and even touched, lepers as well as other "unclean" people (e.g., Matthew 8:1–3; 9:20–22; 10:8; 11:5; 26:6). He served and engaged with the poor, the oppressed, people with infirmities (who were generally deemed to be afflicted by God), and women—even women with shameful pasts (John 4:7–26). In all these ways Jesus was foreshadowing the solidarity with sinners and outsiders he most fully displays on the cross.

No wonder John sums up Jesus' revelation of God by saying "God is love" while defining "love" by the cross.

The cross in John's gospel

The gospel of John tells the story of Jesus a little different than the synoptic gospels, but the centrality of the cross is just as pronounced. In one crucial passage, Jesus says,

> "Now my soul is troubled, and what shall I say? 'Father, save me from this hour'? No it was for this very reason I came to this hour. Father, glorify your name!" Then a voice came from heaven, "I have glorified it, and will glorify it again." (John 12:27–28)

Though his soul is "troubled," Jesus says he will not pray for the Father to save him from "this hour." Throughout John's Gospel, "the hour" refers to Jesus' crucifixion (e.g., 2:4; 7:30; 8:20). And Jesus says he will not pray to avoid his crucifixion because it was "for this very reason" that he had "come to this hour." In other words, this is the principal reason "the Word became flesh." Moreover, as Jesus' prayer makes clear, this "hour" is also the moment when the Father would be most fully glorified.

Immediately following this, Jesus goes on to say, "Now is the time for judgment on this world; now the prince of this world will be driven out. And I, when I am lifted up from the earth, will draw all people to myself" (John 12:31–34). And in case anyone missed it, John adds: "He said this to show the kind of death he was going to die" (12:33).

According to this passage, the world gets judged, the devil gets expelled, and all people get drawn to Christ. The cross accomplished all that—which is to say, the cross accomplished all that needed to be accomplished for the world to be saved.

The centrality of the cross is reflected in other ways in the gospel of John as well. We see its centrality in John's motif of the son of man being "lifted up" (3:14 and 8:28), referring to his crucifixion (John 12:23–24) in conjunction with the "I am" statements that echo God's name in Exodus 3:14 (John 6:20; 8:24, 58; 13:19; 18:5–8). According to Richard Bauckham, the way John combines these two motifs implies that "when Jesus is lifted up, exalted in his humiliation on the cross, then the unique divine identity ('I am he') will be revealed for all who can see."[7] The central point of Jesus' revelation of God concerns his self-sacrificial character, revealed most fully on the cross.

In addition, we can discern the cruciform character of the God reflected in Jesus' self-sacrificial actions in John's gospel. Perhaps the most poignant is when Jesus washes his disciples' feet (John 13:1–5). John tells us that this act demonstrated that Jesus "loved his own who were in the world, he loved them to the end" (v. 1). What makes this act of service even more profound is that John tells us it took place when "the devil had already prompted Judas, the son of Simon Iscariot, to betray Jesus" (v. 2). Jesus humbly serves the one who will betray him, which is precisely what God is doing when he gives his life for the very people who were crucifying him.

Just prior to this act John notes that "Jesus knew that the Father had put all things under his power, and that he had come from God and was returning to God." (v. 3). In fact, John says that this is precisely why Jesus "got up from the meal, took off his outer clothing, and wrapped a towel around his waist" and "began to wash his disciples' feet, drying them with the towel that was wrapped around him" (vv. 4–5). What do you do when you know that "all things" have been placed "under [your] power"? Jesus' answer is, *you serve*.

Colin Gunton insightfully weaves together this episode with the theme of Jesus glorifying the Father by being "lifted up" when he writes, "[The glory of Christ is] the glory of one who washes the feet of his disciples, is lifted up on the cross, and only through the trial of death is elevated to the glory that is reigning with the Father."[8] It is important to realize this if we are to understand what kind of Father is revealed by the incarnate Son. If it is indeed true that those who have seen Jesus have seen the Father, then it is the Father who is revealed in the humanity of the Son and who is most fully glorified through his self-sacrificial death.

The centrality of the cross in Paul's epistles

The centrality of the cross is arguably even more pronounced in Paul's writings than in the Gospels. "Hardly a page goes by in Paul without some reference to Jesus' death," N. T. Wright notes.[9] Consider, for starters, the early Christian hymn found in Philippians 2:6–11, which we mentioned in the previous chapter (vv. 5–8 shared here):

> In your relationships with one another, have the same
>   mindset as Christ Jesus:
>
>> Who, being in very nature God,
>>   did not consider equality with God something to be
>>   used to his own advantage;
>> rather, he made himself nothing
>>   by taking the very nature of a servant,

>   being made in human likeness.
> And being found in appearance as a man,
>   he humbled himself
>   by becoming obedient to death—
>   even death on a cross!

This hymn provides the most direct insight into what Paul and the early church thought about the portrait of God revealed through the cross. In Christ, God "made himself nothing" (*kenosis*) by "taking the very nature of a servant" and "becoming obedient to death—even death on the cross." And it was for this reason, the hymn goes on to proclaim, that the Father "exalted him to the highest place" (v. 9). In short, the God portrayed in this ancient hymn is a God who is exalted by pouring himself out in love to the point of death—"even death on a cross." In the words of Gordon Fee: "Here is where the one who is 'equal with God' has most fully revealed the truth about God: that God is love and that his love expresses itself in self-sacrifice."[10]

The depth of one's love is disclosed by the depth of sacrifice one is willing to make on behalf of the beloved. The unsurpassable sacrifice of God on the cross reveals the unsurpassable perfection of the love that God has for us, and that God eternally is. As Paul says elsewhere, "God demonstrates his own love for us in this: While we were still sinners, Christ died for us" (Romans 5:8).

The centrality of the cross found in this early church hymn reverberates throughout Paul's other writings. For instance, Paul's epistles contain a number of passages that briefly summarize his understanding of the gospel, sometimes referred to as "mini-Gospels."[11] One such passage is Colossians 2:13–15: "When you were dead in your sins and in the uncircumcision of your flesh, God made you alive with Christ. He forgave us all our sins, having canceled the charge of our legal indebtedness, which stood against us and condemned us; he has taken it away, nailing it to the cross. And having disarmed the powers and authorities, he made a public spectacle of them, triumphing over them by the cross."

By means of the cross, God has made us alive, forgiven our sins, canceled our debt and condemnation, disarmed the powers and triumphed over them. For Paul, everything God needed to accomplish to reconcile humanity and the rest of creation back to God was accomplished on the cross. And this same cross-centered emphasis is reflected in each of Paul's "mini-Gospels."

The cross is so central to Paul that he sometimes speaks as if it was the total content of the gospel he preaches. For example, Paul several times speaks of those who oppose his "gospel" as enemies "of the cross" (Philippians 3:18; compare Galatians 6:12). The same identification of "gospel" and "cross" is evident when Paul tells the Corinthians that he and his apostolic team "preach Christ crucified" (1 Corinthians 1:23) as well as when Paul uses the "gospel" and "the message of the cross" interchangeably (1 Corinthians 1:17–18). Given this identification, we ought not be surprised when Paul confesses to the Corinthians that he "resolved to know nothing while I was among you except Jesus Christ and him crucified" (1 Corinthians 2:2). The statement presupposes that everything Paul had to teach is summed up in the message of the cross.

Similarly, in Paul's view, the cross is how the devil is defeated and the creation is set free from his oppressive reign (1 Corinthians 2:8; Colossians 2:14–15). It is how humans are reconciled to God (Romans 5:10), reconciled to each other (Ephesians 2:16), made righteous (Romans 5:19), and transformed and empowered to live in Christ (Romans 6:6; 2 Corinthians 13:4). In fact, Paul declares that the way God was able to "reconcile to himself all things, whether things on earth or things in heaven" was "by making peace through his blood, shed on the cross" (Colossians 1:20). For Paul, as with the gospel of John, the cross is at the heart of everything God is about in our world.

Perhaps the most stunning teaching on the cross in Paul's writings is found in another one of his "mini-Gospels." "For the message of the cross is foolishness to those who are perishing, but to us who are being saved it is the power of God" (1 Corinthians 1:18, compare 1:24).

To people who consider the cross from a "human point of view" (2 Corinthians 5:16 NRSVue), nothing could look weaker than an accused helpless criminal hanging on a cross, and nothing could look more foolish than someone choosing to get crucified when they could have avoided it. And yet, Paul declares that Jesus' crucifixion reveals "the power of God."

The import of what Paul is saying is that, when God flexes God's omnipotent bicep, it doesn't look like Zeus throwing thunderbolts. It looks like Jesus offering up his life for humanity and all creation. It is apparent that for Paul, the cross is not merely "God's means of achieving salvation" but also "a paradigm for God's action in the world," as Graham Tomlin notes. "God gets things done not by a conventional human use of power, by displays of force, but by the kind of self-giving love expressed on Calvary."[12]

This means that the power God relies on to run the cosmos, steer history, and ultimately defeat evil is not a cosmic version of the kind of power after which humans have always lusted. It is rather the power that we earlier saw Jesus allude to when he said, "And I, when I am lifted up from the earth, will draw all people to myself" (John 12:32). The power of God is the power of his self-giving love displayed on Calvary to draw people to Christ and to reconcile all things to himself.

N. T. Wright captures the radical nature of Paul's revelation when he observes that the apostle's theology of the cross "will strain all our categories [for thinking and speaking about God] to the breaking point and beyond." For in light of this central revelation he explains that, "the meaning of the word 'God' includes not only Jesus, but, specifically, the crucified Jesus."[13]

One way we can discern the divine inspiration behind Paul's cross-centered conception of God's power is that it runs counter to nearly everything humanity has ever thought or said about God—or the gods. Across history, people have consistently projected onto their deities the kind of power they themselves have always craved: the power to protect their tribe or nation from enemies and to impose their will on others. Indeed, it has typically been the superior power of deities—not their character—that most fundamentally distinguishes them from humans.

Religion, for the most part, has revolved around humanity's attempts to strike a bargain with these gods: offering sacrifices or adhering to prescribed rituals and rules in exchange for divine favor, prosperity, and military victory. Whether it required sacrificing a firstborn child or scrupulously obeying complex regulations, the goal was always the same—ensuring the deity's power was deployed on one's behalf.

In stark contradiction to this, Paul proclaims that God's power is most fully revealed when Jesus humbles himself, sets aside all divine privileges, becomes fully human, and obeys the Father to the point of death on a cross. As Jürgen Moltmann puts it, "Faith in the Crucified God is . . . a contradiction of everything men have ever conceived, desired and sought to be assured of by the term 'God.'"[14]

This teaching is so radically counterintuitive that, when it came to understanding God's power, providence, and sovereignty, much of the church's theological tradition simply missed it. Instead, many defaulted to the world's familiar equation of power with control. A striking example of this can be found in the *Westminster Confession of Faith*, which declares:

"God from all eternity did, by the most wise and holy counsel of his own will, freely and unchangeably ordain whatsoever comes to pass."[15]

In this view, God's omnipotence, providence, and sovereignty are understood to mean that everything in history conforms to God's eternally unchanging will. Daniel Migliori critiques this conception of divine power, which he labels "godalmightiness," as "simply the greatest power imaginable." While this view has dominated scholastic and Reformed theology, Migliori argues that "the cross of Christ will not fit into this speculative scheme." On the contrary, the cross "demands a complete overhaul of our thinking about power."[16]

The cross and book of Revelation

Turning to the book of Revelation, I should first note that many assume that this work presents a violent Jesus. Mark Driscoll expressed this perspective when, in a 2006 interview, he described Jesus in Revelation as "a pride fighter with a tattoo down His leg, a sword in His hand and the commitment to make someone bleed."[17]

There is no denying that this apocalyptic and prophetic work is filled with violent images and that this violence is associate with "the wrath of the Lamb" (Revelation 6:16). And there is no denying that, if a person understands this work to be a literal snapshot into the final few years of world history, as many evangelicals do, then we must accept that it presents a Jesus who is radically different from the Jesus of the Gospels precisely because he appears so violent.

I consider this way of interpreting Revelation to be misguided. Like other apocalyptic works, Revelation is filled with surrealistic word pictures that are quite absurd if interpreted literally. John is not attempting to provide esoteric information about the final several years of world history. He is rather employing imaginative symbols to alter his audience's understanding of their own world as a means of motivating them to live differently. This is why he tells his first century audience that the things he's writing about will happen "soon," and warns them that "the time is near" (1:1, 3; 22:6–7, 10).

Our job is to try to understand Revelation the way John's first-century audience would have understood it. When we do this, we'll find that John has masterfully taken violent images from the Old Testament and other apocalyptic literature and turned them on their head. In other words, these violent images become violently *anti*-violent.[18]

The centrality of the cross is reflected in a number of different ways in Revelation, three of which I'll now discuss.

First, in the throne-room scene in chapters 4 and 5, a "mighty angel" asks, "Who is worthy to break the seals and open the scroll" (5:2). John hears one of the elders say, "See, the Lion of the tribe of Judah, the Root of David, has triumphed. He is able to open the scroll and its seven seals" (5:5). Anchored in Scripture (see Genesis 49:9; Isaiah 11:1–5), this Lion had become a common, militaristic, triumphant understanding of the messiah.

But then John shocks his audience when he reveals that this Lion is also, at the same time, a little Lamb who had already been slaughtered (5:6). In identifying the Lion as the little Lamb who freely gave his life for a race of rebels, John has subverted the violence associated with the traditional image of the Lion while transforming our understanding about the kind of power God relies on to run the world and to overcome evil.

Yes, the Lion of the tribe of Judah valiantly fights enemies, but he does so not by relying on violence to tear them apart, the way a lion would. He rather does so by refusing to engage in violence against them, choosing instead to lay down his life for them. The scene in the throne room sets the stage for all that will follow in Revelation. All the battles that follow flesh out what it looks like for the Lamb to wage war through the power of the self-sacrificial love of God, revealed most perfectly on the cross.

Second, it is significant that John identifies the slain Lamb with God throughout Revelation. Turning back to Revelation 5, for example, John sees the slain Lamb "standing at the center of the throne" (v. 6). This is the throne on which God sits (e.g., Revelation 4:2–3), and while it's a bizarre image if interpreted literally, it powerfully communicates that the slain Lamb is at the center of who God is and all God does.

Not only this, but the slain Lamb has "seven eyes" and "seven horns" (5:6), depicting the fullness of divine wisdom and power. By associating God's omniscience and omnipotence with the slaughtered Lamb, John has radically transformed standard assumptions about God's sovereignty. As Mitchell Reddish notes, in Revelation, "God's control over the universe is exemplified in the sacrificial, suffering work of the Lamb, not in coercive domination."[19] In the words of G. B. Caird, John has transformed a standard conception of omnipotence as "the power of unlimited coercion" into omnipotence as "the invincible power of self-negating, self-sacrificial love."[20]

A third illustration of the centrality of the cross in Revelation concerns the climactic battle scene found in chapter 19. Some have argued that this chapter contains the most graphic violence in the entire Bible. I will argue that, on closer examination, it becomes clear that it does not.

"The beast and the kings of the earth and their armies" had come to wage war against Jesus and the "armies of heaven" (vv. 14, compare 19). Interestingly, John sees Jesus, riding on his white war horse, "dipped in blood" (v. 13). Don't imagine a mere corner of Jesus' robe being dipped in blood. The entire robe had been dunked (*bapto*) in blood. This gruesome imagery has been adopted from Isaiah 63:3, where Yahweh is depicted as returning from battle splattered with blood and saying, "I trampled them [the nations] in my anger and trod them down in my wrath; their blood spattered my garments, and I stained all my clothing,"

In the ancient Near East, returning from a battle covered in blood was a badge of honor. It was a declaration that the returning warrior had shed his enemies' blood, but his enemies had proven unable to shed his.

As he does throughout Revelation, John takes this violent biblical imagery and ingeniously reverses its meaning. For the mighty warrior in Revelation 19 is soaked in blood *before* he enters into battle. And this is because the blood Jesus is soaked in is not the blood of his enemies—he is drenched in his own blood. This is John's way of telling us that Jesus wages war not by shedding the blood of his enemies, but by allowing his own blood to be shed on behalf of his enemies.

Along the same lines, this mighty warrior shows up for battle riding on a white war horse with "the armies of heaven" behind him (Revelation 19:14). It's a peculiar army, however. The soldiers aren't dressed in military outfits; they're dressed in "fine linen, white and clean" (v. 14). And they are completely unarmed! They don't need weapons, because they never do any fighting. The only weapon the heavenly army relies on is a "sharp sword" that comes out of Jesus' mouth with which he uses to "strike down the nations" (v. 15). And he succeeds! All the kings of the earth—who are the villains throughout Revelation—and all their armies are "killed with the sword coming out of the mouth of the rider on the horse, and all the birds gorged themselves on their flesh" (v. 21).

It looks as if these rebel kings have been brutally slaughtered by Jesus—though the fact that all the kings of the earth were slain by a single sword coming out of Jesus' mouth should tip us off that something other than literal killing is being described here. And our suspicion is confirmed two chapters later where we find these once slain rebel kings alive and well and bringing the splendor of their nations into the heavenly city (Revelation 21:24). What is going on?

It helps to know that throughout Revelation, the Lamb, whose name is "Faithful and True" (19:11, compare 3:14; 15:3; 22:5–6), battles against "the ancient serpent called the devil, or Satan, who leads the whole world astray" (12:9). By means of the beast, which symbolizes the political wing of the serpent's empire, he deceives "the inhabitants of the earth" (13:14, and see 16:13–14; 18:23; 20:8, 10). Indeed, John reminds us that deception is at the core of the battle in Revelation 19 when he notes that the beast and the false prophet "had deluded those who had received the mark of the beast" (v. 20).[21]

In this light, it is apparent that Jesus' mouth-wielding sword did not strike down actual people. What Jesus slaughtered was the false identity of these kings, and "all the inhabitants of the earth" who had received "the mark of the beast." Jesus slaughters all deception by speaking and being the truth. And the truth he speaks is the same truth that is symbolized by his blood-soaked garment. The truth is that the slain Lamb has shed his own blood on behalf of these rebel kings, and it is by this shed blood that they will ultimately be transformed into kings who contribute to the glory of the heavenly city. These kings have come to "know the truth," and it has "set [them] free" (John 8:32).

This battle scene, which at first glance seems so ghastly, turns out, on closer examination, to be a magnificent symbol of the liberating power of the cross.

Jesus' cross-centered ministry is not one revelation among many others in Scripture; rather, as the Word of God, the crucified Christ is the total content of God's revelation. As such, the cross must be considered the filter through which all of our own mental conceptions of God, and all biblical conceptions of God, must be assessed.

Let's now turn to an exploration of how the cross transforms our understanding of depictions of God in Scripture that seem to contradict the revelation of God in the crucified Christ.

3

Cross-Tinted Glasses

Only a person who is aware of the crucified Christ can properly understand Scripture.
—**MARTIN LUTHER**, *TABLE TALK*

There are numerous depictions of God in the Old Testament that are loving and beautiful and that reflect the same divine character we find in Christ. Yahweh is celebrated as a compassionate, nurturing father (Psalm 103:13), a tender comforting mother (Isaiah 49:15; 66:13), a loving husband (Hosea 2:19–20), a gentle shepherd (Isaiah 40:11; Psalm 23), a righteous judge (Psalm 7:11) and as a forgiving lover (Exodus 34:6–7), to name just a few.

At the same time, once we are convinced that God looks like Jesus, we have to honestly confront all the biblical depictions of God that, to one degree or another, do not reflect the other-oriented loving character of God that is revealed on the cross. For example, Yahweh is depicted as wiping out almost the entire human race (Genesis 6:7); drowning Pharaoh's army in the Red Sea (Exodus 15:4); slaughtering thousands by having the earth swallow them, or with plagues, fires, or diseases (Numbers 16:32, 35, 46, 49); slaughtering children and parents by smashing them together (Jeremiah 13:14); commanding Israelites to slaughter their neighbors (Exodus 32:27); commanding capital punishment for an assortment of sexual crimes, including fornication, adultery (20:10) and homosexuality (20:13); smiting a man for trying to keep the ark of the covenant from toppling over (2 Samuel 6:6–7), and, most disturbing of all, commanding the wholescale genocide of populations within the land of Canaan as an act of devotion to God (Deuteronomy 7:1–2).

What are we to make of such macabre divine portraits, especially considering the New Testament's emphatic proclamation that God looks like Jesus?[1]

Two responses

The most common approach to Scripture's troubling portraits of God has been to assume that, since these portraits are part of God's inspired story, they all must be completely accurate. This approach produces a composite and conflicted portrait of God that partly looks like Jesus, yet also partly does not. And the truly tragic consequence of this is that this can't help but compromise the beauty and veracity of people's mental image of God, which in turn negatively impacts the depth of their love for God as well as the depth of their spiritual transformation.

There are other practical ramifications of embracing this composite picture of God as well. Numerous studies have demonstrated that when violent depictions of God are found in literature that a people group considers to carry divine authority, it tends to incline these people toward violence, Christians included.[2] Kenton Sparks notes that throughout history, "Jewish and Christian readers of the Bible have used these texts to justify wholesale, violent, exterminations of their enemies."[3] Joseph Lynch reminds us that the religious massacres of the Medieval period are simply "not comprehensible without factoring in the Old Testament, which permeated not just the language but also the self-view and behavior of the warriors."[4] The same holds true for the church-sanctioned violence against the Indigenous people of North America during the European conquest of this continent.[5]

As people who are called to be peacemakers (Matthew 5:9), "ministers of reconciliation," and "ambassadors" of the kingdom (2 Corinthians 5: 18–20), the problem we are wrestling with could not be more important.

There are many more progressive-minded Christians who avoid this problem by simply dismissing the Scripture's violent divine portraits as mere reflections of the barbaric ancient Near Eastern culture the Hebrews were immersed in. This certainly solves the problem, but it creates another. Jesus clearly and emphatically affirmed the divine inspiration of the Old Testament, and if we confess him to be Lord, I don't see how we can reserve for ourselves the right to correct his theology, especially on such a foundational matter. Moreover, the church has always followed the precedent set by Jesus and the New Testament and confessed the full inspiration of both the Old and New Testaments.

Whatever else this entails, it means that we are not free to simply dismiss any biblical material, including especially its violent depictions of God. We are rather called to wrestle with them. And here is what our wrestling looks like. On the one hand, if we accept that the Bible is divinely inspired, we can't simply dismiss its sub-Christlike depictions of God. On the other hand, if we accept that Jesus is the full revelation of God, neither can we simply accept the Bible's sub-Christlike depictions of God. It's a conundrum, and it's about the get a whole lot worse.

All Scripture is about Jesus

Jesus not only endorsed the Old Testament as divinely inspired, he taught that it was all inspired to ultimately bear witness to him.

In John 5, Jesus chastises the Pharisees by saying, "You study the Scriptures diligently because you think that in them you have eternal life. These are the very Scriptures that testify about me, yet you refuse to come to me to have life" (vv. 39–40). Jesus is teaching that all the diligent study of Scripture in the world will not lead to eternal life unless this study leads people to him. He reiterates the point a few sentences later when he says to his opponents, "If you believed Moses, you would believe me, for he wrote about me. But since you do not believe what he wrote, how are you going to believe what I say?" (vv. 46–47).

According to Jesus, we aren't really believing Moses if we don't realize that he was writing about Jesus. It's apparent that Jesus considered himself the ultimate subject matter of the writings of Moses as well as the rest of the Old Testament.

The point is made even more forcefully in the gospel of Luke when the resurrected Jesus encounters two discouraged disciples walking on the road to Emmaus. These disciples told Jesus how distraught they were over the death of the one they had hoped was the Messiah (Luke 24:19–24). Jesus then replies, "'How foolish you are, and how slow to believe all that the prophets have spoken! Did not the Messiah have to suffer these things and then enter his glory?' And beginning with Moses and all the Prophets, he explained to them what was said in all the Scriptures concerning himself" (Luke 24:25–27).

All Scripture, Jesus claims, is about him, and especially about the need for him to "suffer these things"—his crucifixion—before entering "his glory." Jesus reiterates the same point later to his disciples. "'This is what I told you while I was still with you: Everything must be fulfilled that is written about me in the Law of Moses, the Prophets and the Psalms.' Then he opened their minds so they could understand the Scriptures. He told them, 'This is what is written: The Messiah will suffer and rise from the dead on the third day'" (Luke 24:44–46).

According to Graeme Goldsworthy and a number of other scholars, Jesus isn't merely claiming that there are splattered verses here and there throughout the Law, the Prophets, and the Psalms that testify to him. Jesus is rather claiming that "the whole Old Testament, not merely a few selected texts, is about him."[6] Similarly, Vern Poythress contends that in this "particularly important" passage, "Christ himself indicates that the Old Testament from beginning to end is about himself" and that "the whole of the Old Testament . . . has as its central message the suffering and resurrection of Christ."[7]

Moreover, since Jesus is "the goal and fulfillment of the whole Old Testament" as well as "the embodiment of the truth of God," Goldsworthy argues that Jesus must be regarded as "the interpretive key to the Bible." Hence, he concludes, the central question every Christian interpreter of the Old Testament must always ask is: "How does this passage of Scripture . . . testify to Christ?"[8]

Finally, in his first letter to the Corinthians, Paul says he passed on to them a tradition he had received, one that was "of first importance." The primary element of this tradition, as a matter of "first importance," was that "Christ died for our sins according to the Scriptures" (1 Corinthians 15:3). It was the same truth Paul passed on to King Agrippa when he said, "I am saying nothing beyond what the prophets and Moses said would happen—that the Messiah would suffer and, as the first to rise from the dead, would bring the message of light to his own people and to the Gentiles" (Acts 26:22–23).

As with the previous two passages, Paul isn't merely claiming that a few isolated verses predicted the Messiah's suffering and death. As Balthasar notes, he is rather claiming that, on the cross, "the whole meaning of that direction in which the nation [of Israel] was led" reaches "its transcendent goal."[9]

Of course, it's not immediately obvious how all Scripture bears witness to Christ's suffering. This is evident in the fact that the disciples could only understand this after Jesus "opened their minds" (Luke 24:45). To discern how all Scripture points to Christ, therefore, we must acknowledge that a strictly exegetical interpretation will not suffice. We need the Spirit of Christ to open our eyes and reveal the deeper, Christ-centered meaning embedded within the text.

Some evangelicals argue that the original author's intended meaning is the only meaning a passage can have. Yet, the New Testament authors clearly did not share this conviction. Under the influence of the Spirit, they consistently looked for, and discovered, Christ in passages which, on a strictly exegetical level, have nothing to do with him.

Take, for example, Hosea 11, where Yahweh declares: "When Israel was a child, I loved him, and out of Egypt I called my son" (v. 1). This passage plainly refers to Yahweh's deliverance of Israel from Egypt, where the Hebrews had been enslaved. Yet, after Mary, Joseph, and Jesus left Egypt to settle in Nazareth, Matthew writes: "And so was fulfilled what the Lord had said through the prophet: 'Out of Egypt I called my son'" (Matthew 2:15).

When Matthew claims that Jesus' departure from Egypt "fulfilled" Hosea's declaration, he is not suggesting that Hosea predicted Jesus' exodus. Instead, he is claiming that Jesus' exodus completes, or "fills out," the meaning of Hosea's oracle. But to discern this meaning, Matthew had to go beyond Hosea's original intended meaning.

This is what we observe throughout the New Testament. In a variety of ways, and under the influence of the Holy Spirit, the authors of the New Testament consistently go beyond the plain exegetical meaning of passages to discern how the passage bears witness to Christ.

Moreover, though the church has been inconsistent in its application, it has always professed that Jesus Christ is the ultimate subject matter of all Scripture and the key to correctly interpreting all Scripture, as Henri de Lubac has demonstrated.[10]

So, our dilemma turns out to be threefold.

- On the authority of Jesus and his church, we must consider all Scripture—including its violent depictions of God—to be divinely inspired.

- On the authority of Jesus' definitive revelation of God, we cannot affirm Scripture's violent depictions of God.

- On the authority of Jesus and Paul, we must consider all Scripture—including its violent depictions of God—to bear witness to Jesus, and more specifically, to Jesus' suffering and death.

Is there a way of reconciling these seemingly contradictory convictions? I believe there is. And I believe the key is found in God's revelation on the cross.

Cruciform power

In chapter 2, we discussed Paul's astounding claim that "the cross . . . is the power of God" (1 Corinthians 1:18). This means that the power of God is the power of other-oriented love. It is not a power that dominates or coerces others but a power that honors the personhood and freedom of others, even when they choose to walk away from God.

While the influential power of cruciform love looks "weak" to those who assume that power and control are synonyms, it's the only kind of power that can accomplish God's primary goal for humanity, which is for us to enter into a loving relationship with God—a relationship that mirrors the eternal loving relationship of the Father, Son, and Spirit (John 17:20–26).

However, although God is by nature perfect love, humans are not. There is a subtle contradiction in supposing that a human, who by nature is contingent (meaning, we could be otherwise than we are), could possess a necessarily loving nature. For humans, love must be chosen.

Thus, while the Spirit tirelessly works to influence people toward the practice of love and truth, she always stops short of coercion.[11] The Spirit does this because, if she were to coerce us into believing only true things and engaging only in godly behavior, our godly thoughts and behavior would not be authentically *ours*, and there would be no possibility of us entering an authentic loving relationship with God. This has significant implications for our understanding of how God inspired the writing of his story.

God's relational "breathing"

In 2 Timothy 3:16, Paul declares, "All Scripture is God-breathed [*theopneustos*] and is useful for teaching, rebuking, correcting and training in righteousness." Since breathing is an activity we ordinarily accomplish entirely on our own, most Christians have assumed that the Bible was "breathed" by God unilaterally, with nothing outside of God conditioning what God's "breathing" produced. And if no outside influences shaped this process, it would follow that the Bible must reflect God's own perfection. In other words, it must be entirely free of mistakes or "inerrant." Whatever teachings are found in Scripture must be received, John Calvin says, "without exception . . . because they have emanated from [God] alone and are mixed with nothing human."[12]

There are an insurmountable number of objections to this perspective, not least of which is that it conflicts with the Bible we have. The Bible we have contains a veritable "encyclopedia" of errors, contradictions, and inaccuracies.[13] But the problem that presently concerns us is that Calvin's line of reasoning presupposes that the Spirit dominated the biblical authors to the point of eliminating all their sin and imperfections so that she could produce a text that reflects God's own perfection.

If, on the other hand, we grant that the Spirit's power is the power of the cross—the power of influential, self-sacrificial love—then we cannot assume that everything we find in Scripture comes directly from the mouth of God. Instead, we can say that, in the process of "breathing" Scripture, the Spirit influenced the authors in the direction of truth *as much as possible* while accommodating their limitations and sin *as much as necessary*.

Therefore, as we read Scripture, we must discern the degree to which any given biblical material reflects the Spirit breaking through versus the degree to which it reflects the limitations and sin of the biblical author suppressing the Spirit. And since all Scripture was breathed for the ultimate purpose of bearing witness to the revelation of God in the crucified Christ, this revelation must be the central criterion by which we make this determination.

Breathing through sin

If we place the cross at the center of our thinking about what it means to be "God-breathed," the concept of God's "breathing" takes on new meaning and the human imperfections we find throughout the Bible cease to be a problem.

On the cross, God "breathed" his definitive self-revelation precisely by making our imperfections his own. Indeed, Paul goes so far as to declare that Christ became our sin (2 Corinthians 5:21) as well as our curse (Galatians 3:13). If God "breathed" the full disclosure of his eternal character through the man who bore all the imperfections of humanity on the cross, how could anyone insist that God's "breathing" must be free from all human imperfections? To the contrary, when interpreted through the lens of the cross, the Bible's human imperfections *contribute to* the beauty of its cross-centered message, as I have argued elsewhere.[14]

To say it differently, if the cross reveals what God is truly like, it reveals what God has *always* been like, in all of God's activities. And it is this God who reveals himself by "breathing" his story. Since God "breathed" his fullest self-revelation by stooping to bear all the sin and imperfections of humanity, should we not *expect* to find God "breathing" through human sin and imperfection in Scripture?

Related to this, if the cross appears "foolish" and "weak" to the natural mind and can only be understood as the "wisdom" and "power" of God to those who have faith, should we not *expect* to find material in Scripture that appears, on the surface, to look "foolish" and "weak" but that unveils a wise and powerful message to those who believe "the message of the cross" (1 Corinthians 1:18, 24)?

Does this mean that we must reject the infallibility of the Bible? It all depends on what you mean by "infallible." The word "infallible" means unfailing, and for something to fail or not fail depends on the standard you are measuring it up against. If the standard is anything other than bearing witness to Jesus Christ, I'm afraid you're going to be disappointed. In fact, I think you're going to be disappointed even if you restrict your standard to uniform theological accuracy.

For example, we instinctively interpret references to Yahweh riding on clouds, throwing down lightning bolts, and the like to be metaphorical (e.g., Psalms 18:14; 68:4; 104:3). But ancient biblical authors, along with everybody else in the ancient Near East, viewed God or the gods as literally doing things like this. They were, to this degree, simply mistaken, products of their ancient Near Eastern culture.

So, by what criteria should we assess the infallible nature of Scripture? I submit that this is precisely what Jesus gives us when he teaches that all Scripture is inspired to bear witness to him, and more specifically, to his sacrificial suffering and death. If we trust Scripture to lead us to Christ, it will not fail us.

How the cross reveals God

I'd now like us to reflect for a moment on how the cross reveals God to us. This question is rarely asked, but I hope to demonstrate that it is a question of supreme importance.

Consider that when first-century Jews viewed the crucified Christ "from a human point of view," as Paul once did (2 Corinthians 5:16 NRSVue), they saw nothing more than a guilty, God-cursed criminal—no different from the countless others crucified by the Romans. This is all that can be seen with the natural eye. So, what enables believers to gaze upon the cross and discern something profoundly more? What is it about the believer's perspective that transforms Jesus' execution into the supreme display of God's cruciform character?

The answer is *faith*. By faith, we perceive something happening behind the scenes of Jesus' crucifixion that sets him apart from every other condemned man. Faith allows us to see beyond the surface to witness God stooping an infinite distance, out of incomprehensible love, to become our sin and our curse in this godforsaken, crucified criminal. And it is the unsurpassable extremity to which God was willing to stoop on our behalf that reveals the unsurpassable perfection of the love that God has for us—and the love that God eternally is. But this revelation only occurs if we trust "the message of the cross," which proclaims that in Christ, God was stooping to bear the sin of the world and to reconcile it to himself (1 Corinthians 1:18).

This is why the cross is both supremely ugly and supremely beautiful to those who behold it with the eyes of faith. On the surface, it is a grotesque spectacle, reflecting the horrifying sin and godforsaken curse that Jesus bore. Yet, to those who by faith peer beyond this grim surface, the cross unveils the ultimate beauty of a God who would humble himself and stoop to such an extreme out of his boundless love for us and creation.

Hence, for those of us who trust the message of the cross, the cross becomes both a mirror of the appalling ugliness of our sin and a radiant revelation of the God who was willing to become this ugliness. In this paradox of divine love and human sin, the cross becomes the supreme intersection of the grotesque and the glorious.

If the cross reveals what God is always like, including what God was like when he "breathed" Scripture, should we not expect to find God stooping to bear the imperfections and sin of his people in the process of "breathing" his story? Should we not expect to encounter material that is revoltingly ugly on the surface, reflecting the sin and imperfections of its human author, but that bears witness to God's accommodating love and cruciform character if we interpret it while exercising faith in "the message of the cross"?

At this point, we can begin to understand how Scripture's violent divine portraits bear witness to the cross. What is going on behind the scenes of these sin-distorted portraits is precisely what was going on behind the scenes of the cross. God was stooping to bear the sin of God's people and therefore taking on a surface appearance that reflects the ugliness of that sin. But again, this can only be seen if we trust fully in the "message of the cross" and are therefore willing to exercise a surface-probing faith that looks behind the scenes.

By contrast, if we do not fully trust Jesus when he says, "Anyone who has seen me has seen the Father" (John 14:9)—if we suspect that it is not outside the character of God to command genocide, for example—then we will not be inclined to exercise faith to see God humbly stooping behind the scenes of such a portrait. Instead of looking through the surface meaning of Moses' violent depiction of God to discern God humbly stooping to bear the sin of his people's fallen misconception of him, we will simply trust the fallen misconception.

We will only be motivated to look deeper if we accept that biblical portraits of God commanding or engaging in violence cannot be accurate, precisely because we trust that God looks like Jesus.

Let's delve into what is arguably the Bible's most challenging depiction of God: Yahweh commanding his people to engage in what can only be described as merciless genocide.

4

Literary Crucifixes

Only because God continually took up the cross in an act of self-denial did God's relationship with the world and with Israel continue. The cross on Golgotha was then the logical end term of the way God had been through the First Testament story.

—**JOHN GOLDINGAY**, *KEY QUESTIONS ABOUT BIBLICAL INTERPRETATION*

Until around twenty years ago, I tirelessly sought explanations for why God might have commanded the Israelites to annihilate entire populations in the land of Canaan, along with the other frightful things ascribed to Yahweh in the Old Testament. I even began writing a book to compile all these explanations. It would have been a book along the lines of Paul Copan's *Is God a Moral Monster?*, in which Copan attempts to rationally justify the violence ascribed to God in the Old Testament. He does as good a job of this as can be done.

Fifty pages into writing my book, I quit. I realized that at best, my explanations could only make God seem a little less arbitrary and cruel. But they did nothing to address the most important challenge we face, which is to disclose how all Scripture, including its violent portraits of God, bears witness to Jesus' sacrificial death.

After abandoning my book project, I spent several months living in the cognitive dissonance created by the threefold dilemma I posed in the previous chapter. During this time, I followed the guidance of my favorite early church theologian, Origen of Alexandria. Origen believed that the Spirit intentionally inserted material which "at first glance" seems "neither . . . true nor useful."[1] Origen considered this material to be God-inspired "stumbling blocks," "interruptions of the historical sense," "impossibilities," and alleged events "that could not have happened at all." By "shutting us out" and "debarring us from the [literal interpretation]," the Holy Spirit motivates us to consider "another way" that "can bring us, through the entrance of a narrow footpath to a higher and loftier road and lay open the immense breath of the divine wisdom." In cases such as these, Origen continues, we are forced to "search for a truth deeper down" as we try to discover in the Scriptures "a meaning worthy of God."[2] We must interpret such problematic passages "not according to the meanness of speech but according to the divinity of the Holy Spirit who inspired them."[3] In my estimation, Origen was simply following the pattern of the New Testament authors in approaching Scripture this way.

Origen believed the Spirit intentionally buried these treasures beneath the surface of "unworthy" biblical material so that

> not everyone who wished should have these mysteries laid before his feet to be trampled on, but that they should be for the man who has devoted himself to studies of this kind with the utmost purity and sobriety and through nights of watching, by which means perchance he might be able to trace out the deeply hidden meaning of the Spirit of God concealed under the language of an ordinary narrative which points in a different direction, and that so

he might become a sharer of the Spirit's knowledge and a partaker of his divine counsel.[4]

The buried treasure of divine wisdom is disclosed only to those who "prove themselves worthy of being taught . . . to know matters of such value and importance."[5]

Like many other Christian thinkers from the first few centuries of the church, Origen understood the violent depictions of God in the Old Testament to be radically inconsistent with the revelation of God in Christ and thus classified these depictions as among the "unworthy" canonical material that debars us from a literal interpretation and forces us to dig for a deeper meaning. Indeed, Origen believed that a literal interpretation of Scripture's violent divine portraits would lead "some of the simpler . . . within the faith of the Church" to "believe such things about [God] as would not be believed even of the most unjust and savage of men."[6]

The way Origen, Gregory of Nyssa, John Cassian, and others in the early church discovered the deeper meaning of problematic biblical material was by interpreting this material allegorically.[7] This was a widely respected method of interpretation at the time, but it is not so regarded today. Yet, while I could not accept the allegorical way Origen and others dug for the hidden meaning of Scripture, my sense was that these early Christian thinkers were moving in the right direction.

Unfortunately, their project was cut short once the church of the fourth century embraced political power, and with it, the use of violence. For once this happened, a literal interpretation of violent divine portraits of God ceased to be problematic and even came to be seen by some as advantageous.[8] When political and religious leaders needed to motivate Christians to conquer new lands, such as when the Europeans invaded the Americas, they could appeal to Old Testament's violent divine portraits as precedent.

Acquiring the magic eye

Then, one day, it happened. The core insight came to me in a flash, though it has taken me years to fully work it out. I personally believe this was a Spirit-inspired revelation, but as one who believes the Bible's interpretation belongs to the church, not to any individual, I must leave this question for the church to determine over time.

I can liken my experience to the first time I encountered a Magic Eye book in the early 1990s, when these books were in vogue. I was at a neighborhood Christmas party, and some folks were passing around one of these books. None of us had seen anything like it before. Each page of the book was filled with what appeared to be nothing more than random patterns. But as the book was passed around, people claimed they could see a three-dimensional picture emerging from each page.

Then it was my turn. One neighbor advised me not to look *at* the page but to look *through* it. I didn't know what that meant, but I tried. Nothing. Another told me to relax my eyes while holding the entire page in view. I didn't know what that meant either, but I spent about fifteen minutes trying. Still nothing. Before long, another neighbor suggested I was "trying too hard." How, I wondered, was I supposed to try *less*?

By the end of the party, I was the only person who had not been able to see the three-dimensional picture everyone else claimed to see. The host of the party, who happened to own the book, graciously lent it to me so I could keep trying. Over the next two weeks, I made multiple attempts to acquire the magic eye for myself and see what others were seeing, but always with the same frustrating results.

Then one evening, as I sat on my couch gazing at the random patterns of a page in this book, I suddenly began to see a three-dimensional object emerge. Initially, I couldn't make out what it was, and my glimpses were fleeting. But eventually, I could clearly see four three-dimensional dolphins rising off the page. I was elated, almost to the point of tears!

That experience was something like what I felt when I first discovered the hidden treasure of the cross buried in the depths of Scripture's violent depictions of God. After months of gazing at this troubling material with the conviction that it must *somehow* point to the cross, I suddenly began to see how it does so.

In this chapter, I'd like to invite you to view Scripture's violent portraits of God in this fashion. I will focus on the Bible's conquest narrative, as this narrative arguably contains the material most at odds with the revelation of God in Christ.[9] My hope is that if readers can come to understand how the ghoulish portrait of God commanding genocide bears witness to the cross, they will, over time, be able to discern this pattern in the Bible's other violent or otherwise immoral divine portraits.

Being honest

The first step in wrestling with the disturbing depictions of God in the Old Testament is to be honest about the material itself. Many Christians instinctively shy away from saying anything negative about the Bible. It is, after all, God's inspired word. Yet, the Bible itself provides numerous examples of faithful people voicing their honest complaints to God when it seemed he was acting out of character—from Job to Jeremiah. None of them were struck down for doing so. God isn't put off by our honesty. What is off-putting to God is when we are not honest.

Let's take an unflinching look at two representative passages that portray Yahweh as commanding genocide.[10] In Deuteronomy 7, Yahweh is depicted as instructing Moses: "When the Lord your God brings you into the land you are entering to possess and drives out before you . . . seven nations larger and stronger than you—and when the Lord your God has delivered them over to you and you have defeated them, then you must destroy them totally [*herem*]. Make no treaty with them, and show them no mercy" (vv. 1–2).

The Hebrew word *herem*, translated here as "destroy them totally," connotes not only annihilating people, but doing so as a sacred duty to Yahweh.[11] It is strikingly like the way Israel's pagan neighbors (and sometimes Israel itself) would sacrifice their firstborn children to their gods, only in this case it is men, women, children, infants, and even animals that Yahweh commanded to be sacrificed. And the Israelites were explicitly commanded to "show them no mercy" as they carried out this calamity. "Compassion was to be avoided at all costs," remarks Kenton Sparks.[12] It could not have been easy to carry out the slaughter as young Canaanite mothers desperately pleaded for their babies to be spared. But a divine order is a divine order, so no mercy was granted.

Can you imagine Jesus, who instructs us to "be merciful, just as your Father is merciful" (Luke 6:36), giving such an order to anyone, for any reason?

The instruction is given in even more detail later in Deuteronomy. In chapter 20, Yahweh first addresses how the Israelites were to deal with cities belonging to Canaanites not included in the seven nations marked for annihilation. If a city resisted Israelite rule, Yahweh commands: "Put to the sword all the men in it. As for the women, the children, the livestock, and everything else in the city, you may take these as plunder for yourselves" (Deuteronomy 20:13–14).

Throughout the ancient Near East, enjoying the spoils of war—including taking captured women as sex slaves—was common practice. There is no reason to think this implication is absent here, for it is made explicit in other biblical contexts (e.g., Numbers 31:17–18).

But these Canaanites were the fortunate ones. The narrative immediately moves on to recount Yahweh's instructions regarding the seven nations whose land he promised to Israel as their inheritance: "However, in the cities of the nations the LORD your God is giving you as an inheritance, do not leave alive anything that breathes. Completely destroy (*herem*) them ... as the LORD your God has commanded you. Otherwise, they will teach you to follow all the detestable things they do in worshiping their gods, and you will sin against the LORD your God" (Deuteronomy 20:16–18).

Curiously, after commanding the Israelites to slaughter every living thing that breathes, Yahweh is depicted as instructing them not to destroy the trees during a siege, rhetorically asking: "Are the trees people, that you should besiege them?" (Deuteronomy 20:19).

While we may be grateful that Yahweh exhibits ecological sensitivity, we must honestly acknowledge that these are truly horrific depictions of God. Were these and similar biblical passages found in the Quran or any other "holy" book outside the Bible, we would denounce them as diabolically genocidal. They do not become less diabolically genocidal simply because we find them in our Bible.

At the same time, because they are included in our God-breathed Scripture, we cannot simply dismiss them. Following Origen's advice, we must instead search for a cross-pointing hidden treasure beneath the diabolically genocidal surface of these passages.

Defending the violent God

Conservative Christian apologists, who are committed to defending the surface meaning of these passages, have offered several explanations as to why Yahweh felt he had to give this grisly command. I'll address the two I consider to be the most plausible explanations.

One argues that God was justified in ordering the extermination of these seven people groups because, as Deuteronomy

20:18 explains, God was concerned the Israelites might "follow all the detestable things they do in worshiping their gods." As terrible as it was, they argue, God knew the long term impact on his people would be even worse.[13]

There are at least four problems with this explanation. First, while archaeological evidence suggests that these people groups practiced barbaric and ungodly rituals, it also indicates that they were no worse than many other groups in Canaan or throughout the ancient Near East. In other words, their barbarity does not explain why Yahweh singled them out for total destruction.

Second, the most detestable practice shared by these groups was the sacrifice of their firstborn children.[14] It is darkly ironic that Yahweh would want to protect the Israelites from this heinous practice by having them engage in something even more detestable—the wholesale slaughter of entire populations as a sacred duty to him.

Third, even if we were to grant that God was justified in commanding such butchery, this would only make him seem a little less arbitrary. It would not make him look more Christlike. The God revealed in Jesus loves indiscriminately—like the sun shining and the rain falling on all alike—and he forbids all violence (Matthew 5:39, 44–45; Luke 6:27–35).

Fourth, and most importantly, even if this explanation were accepted, it would yet fail to disclose how these horrific portraits of God bear witness to the suffering and death of Jesus, as Jesus claimed all Scripture is meant to do (Luke 24:27–30).

Yahweh was speaking hyperbolically

Another explanation has gained traction among evangelical apologists. In *Is God a Moral Monster?*, Paul Copan contends that Yahweh's commands to destroy entire populations are examples of ancient Near Eastern hyperbolic "war bravado." According to Copan, these accounts employ exaggerated language typical of the time, much like a sports team claiming they "totally destroyed" their opponent without implying literal annihilation. Copan writes, "The sweeping language of total obliteration was typically hyperbolic, common to ancient Near Eastern warfare accounts. It conveyed victory, not literal destruction."[15]

There are three problems with this explanation.

While it's true that ancient Near Eastern kings and military leaders frequently employed exaggerated "war bravado"—where macabre violence against enemies was seen as a badge of honor—one would hope the Creator of heaven and earth would rise above such destructively juvenile talk.

Moreover, as with the argument that destruction was justified, even if we were to accept this explanation of hyperbolic language, it at best makes Yahweh appear a bit less monstrous. He doesn't demand genocide, but he still wants a lot of people killed. It does little, however, to make this divine portrait compatible with the God revealed in Christ. Still less does this perspective help demonstrate how this violent depiction bears witness to the cross.

Finally, here is one of two scriptural accounts that suggest that the *herem* command was intended literally.[16] In Numbers 31, Yahweh is depicted as instructing Moses to take vengeance on the Midianites (v. 2). Moses sent troops to attack this doomed ethnic group, and they "burned all the towns where the Midianites had settled, as well as all their camps" (v. 10). Yet when the soldiers returned from battle, Moses was enraged (v. 14). Why? Because they had only slaughtered the adult men (v. 15)!

In response, Moses commanded them, "Kill all the boys and kill every woman who has slept with a man. But save for yourselves every girl who has never slept with a man" (vv. 17–18). As mentioned above, in the context of the ancient Near East, "save for yourselves" meant the soldiers were permitted to take the virgins as spoils of war—including as sex slaves.

In any event, it seems clear Moses interpreted Yahweh's call for "vengeance" as a command for literal annihilation—though he apparently decided to boost the morale of his soldiers by allowing them to keep virgin girls alive as a reward for their victory. And if Moses understood *herem* literally in this instance, on what basis can anyone claim it was hyperbolic in other instances?

Hearing what we expect to hear

Two more points will help set the stage for our exploration of a cruciform interpretation of the genocidal portrait of God.

The first concerns the well-documented phenomenon of confirmation bias. This is the tendency for people to interpret what they see and hear in ways that confirm what they already want and expect to see and hear. While this phenomenon has been thoroughly established in scientific studies over the past half-century, it is also attested throughout the biblical narrative. Let me highlight several examples.

Like most Jews of their time, Jesus' disciples expected the Messiah to overthrow their oppressors and restore Israel to its former glory. So, when Jesus repeatedly spoke of his impending arrest, suffering, and death, it went in one ear and out the other. Peter even went so far as to rebuke Jesus for speaking this way (Matthew 16:21–22). Consequently, when these events unfolded exactly as Jesus had predicted, the disciples were shocked. It was only after the resurrection, and only when the Spirit opened their eyes, that they could remember and comprehend that Jesus had been trying to prepare them for this all along.

In Psalm 18, the psalmist reflects how people's perceptions of God are influenced by the state of their hearts. "To the faithful you show yourself faithful, to the blameless you show yourself blameless, to the pure you show yourself pure, but to the devious you show yourself shrewd" (Psalm 18:25–26; 2 Samuel 22:26–27).

The Hebrew word for "devious" (*iqqesh*) is sometimes translated as "crooked" or "perverted," while the word for "shrewd" (*pathal*) can also mean "deceptive." Both words carry the connotation of something being twisted. The psalmist is stating that God appears faithful, blameless, and pure to those whose hearts are faithful, blameless, and pure. But to those whose hearts are twisted, God appears in twisted ways. This expresses the ancient insight, found throughout the Bible, that *like is known by like.*

Similar to a Rorschach test, the way people perceive God reveals as much about their own hearts as it does about God. This principle is also central to the teachings of Jesus. He frequently emphasized that people can only understand spiritual truths when their hearts are aligned with God.

For example, in chapter 2 of this book, we discussed how Jesus rebuked the Pharisees for diligently studying Scripture while failing to find the "life" it offers, because they didn't recognize that all Scripture points to him (John 5:39–40, 45–47). Jesus explained their failure bluntly: "I know you . . . you do not have the love of God in your hearts" (John 5:42). The condition of one's heart clearly affects what they can, and cannot, understand.

Later, Jesus confronted another group of people who continually misunderstood him. He asked, "Why is my language not clear to you?" He then answered his own question: "Because you are unable to hear what I say. You belong to your father, the devil, and you want to carry out your father's desires" (John 8:43–44). Clearly, the condition of one's heart determines what they can and cannot comprehend.

Finally, when the disciples asked Jesus why he spoke in parables, he explained: "Because the knowledge of the secrets of the kingdom of heaven has been given to you, but not to them" (Matthew 13:11).

Jesus then applied a prophecy from Isaiah to explain why others could not understand his parables: "You will be ever hearing but never understanding; you will be ever seeing but never perceiving. For this people's heart has become calloused; they hardly hear with their ears, and they have closed their eyes. Otherwise they might see with their eyes, hear with their ears, understand with their hearts and turn, and I would heal them" (Matthew 13:14–15; compare Isaiah 6:9–10).

Jesus made it clear that an individual's hard-heartedness renders them incapable of grasping spiritual truths or turning to him for healing.

This biblical motif is particularly relevant to our study because of a recurring theme in the Old Testament: the Israelites were consistently described as a stiff-necked and spiritually dull people. Let me emphasize that this is not intended to single out ancient Israel as uniquely sinful. To the contrary, we should consider Israel to be a microcosm of the human race. Scripture teaches that, apart from God's grace, we are all "dead in [our] transgressions and sins" (Ephesians 2:1). I highlight Israel's hard-heartedness only to underscore how it should caution us against assuming their understanding and experience of God—and, therefore, their depictions of God—were consistently accurate.

This refrain about the Israelites' inability to know God clearly is woven throughout the Old Testament. For example, the Lord laments through the prophet Jeremiah: "My people are fools; they do not know me. They are senseless children; they have no understanding. They are skilled in doing evil; they know not how to do good" (Jeremiah 4:22).

Similarly, Hosea declares: "There is no faithfulness, no love, no acknowledgment of God in the land" (Hosea 4:1). While

I assume there is an element of hyperbole in both of these oracles, they nevertheless paint a spiritually grim picture. And given that spiritually twisted hearts inevitably experience God in twisted ways, it should not surprise us to find distorted images of God within the biblical narrative.

What should surprise us—and fill us with awe—is how frequently and beautifully the Spirit broke through Israel's hard-heartedness. Time and again, God was able to grant the Israelites—and by extension, all of us—glimpses of his true nature and will. These glimpses find their ultimate expression in the cross-centered life and ministry of Jesus.

While it requires the surface-penetrating vision of a cross-informed faith to discern how God stooped to bear his people's sin when biblical portraits fall short of the character revealed in Jesus, we must also celebrate the Spirit-inspired truth and beauty that saturates the Old Testament.

The God who humbly accommodates

Throughout Scripture, God mercifully stoops to accommodate people's nonideal circumstances. This divine condescension is a profound expression of God's humility and love, and should influence a cross-centered approach to interpreting divine violence. Let me offer a few examples.

From the beginning, God's ideal for marriage was lifelong monogamy (Genesis 2:22–25). When women and children were being left without a provider or protector due to men dying in war, however, God bent this ideal to allow for polygamy. Similarly, Jesus explained that "because your hearts were hard," God permitted divorce, though he placed regulations around it to protect the wives who were being cast aside (Matthew 19:8–9; compare Deuteronomy 24:1–4). These concessions reveal God's willingness to meet his people where they were, even when it meant accommodating their fallen, culturally conditioned practices.

Similarly, God's original plan for Israel was to be a nation without a human king—a theocracy in which Yahweh alone would reign as King. It was one of the ways Yahweh hoped his people would be "a light for the Gentiles" (e.g., Isaiah 42:6–7; 49:6). However, trusting in an invisible King proved challenging for a people surrounded by hostile neighbors. Eventually, the Israelites demanded a human king, saying: "We want . . . [to] be like all the other nations, with a king to lead us and to go out before us and fight our battles" (1 Samuel 8:19–20).

Yahweh viewed this request as a rejection of his kingship (1 Samuel 8:7). He even warned the Israelites about the burdens a human king would impose (1 Samuel 8:11–18). Yet, the Israelites persisted, so Yahweh obliged them.

What makes this example particularly interesting is that, in the ancient Near East, kings were typically viewed as mediators between their national deity and the people. Once Yahweh granted Israel's request for a king, he began to take on the appearance of a typical ancient Near Eastern deity in the biblical narrative—working through kings to accomplish his will.

There are many other instances of Yahweh stooping to accommodate his people's fallen beliefs and practices, including animal sacrifices and relating to his people through the law. In each case, Yahweh appears to condone these practices, though in truth he was graciously meeting his people where they were in order to stay in relationship with them and gradually reveal his true character to them.

Each accommodation reflects God's humble willingness to bear the sin and limitations of his people, just as he does in a superlative way on the cross. In stooping to accommodate human fallenness, God takes on the appearance of a deity who approves of the very practices he is tolerating. Yet, this is not approval; it is a profound act of divine humility and love. And each accommodation points forward to the ultimate expression of God's humility and self-sacrificial love, when God stooped to bear the sin and curse of the world and thus took on a sinful and cursed appearance.

This pattern of divine accommodation provides a key framework for understanding how macabre portraits of God in Scripture can ultimately bear witness to the God revealed in Christ.

A cruciform understanding of *herem*

With these two points established, we can now explore how to find the crucified Christ in Moses' genocide-commanding portrait of Yahweh.

To begin, if we fully trust that God looks like Jesus and has always looked like Jesus, then I do not see how we can also think Moses heard the Lord correctly when he thought Yahweh said, "Kill everything that breathes." We have to conclude that Moses was mistaken.

From my own experience, I know how challenging it initially can be to consider disagreeing with a biblical author's portrayal of the Almighty if you've been taught that the Bible has no errors. Cognitive dissonance is not fun! But I also know how freeing it can be to no longer feel you have to accept that the unconditionally loving God whom you've come to know and love in Jesus Christ once wanted his people to mercilessly slaughter untold numbers of children and infants—along with everyone and everything else that "breathes." Many others have experienced this liberation as well.

Several months before my book *Crucifixion of the Warrior God* was released in 2018, I preached a four-part sermon series presenting much of the material I've discussed here, along with additional confirming evidence for this cruciform interpretation that I will discuss shortly. At the conclusion of the final service in this series, a dear woman, a longtime member of the church I pastor, approached me. Her face was soaked with tears, and her strong emotions made it difficult for her to speak.

She tried several times to say something but could only choke on her words. Then, suddenly, she rushed forward and gave me a tight bear hug, clinging to me for what felt like ten or fifteen seconds.

When she finally composed herself, she said, "When I found Jesus, I felt like I had found *the man of my dreams*. I've loved him for over fifty years. But until today, I could never bring myself to completely trust him or give him my whole heart. I felt like a wife who discovered her beloved husband had once gunned down a classroom full of children. I could never fully trust someone who was capable of such heartless violence, for any reason, or however long ago, and regardless of how perfect he'd been since."

She then grabbed my hands, her tear-filled eyes locking onto mine. Her voice, strained with emotion but resolute, continued: "Today, I learned my beloved Jesus never did such a thing. Today, I can give him my whole heart, and it feels so good!" With that, she pulled me into another bear hug, this one even longer and tighter than before.

What a magnificent example of how the way we envision God determines how we feel about him. Any suspicion that there may be a sinister side of God, however long ago he may have displayed it, will compromise your love and devotion toward God. And what a poignant reminder to hold fast to this all-important truth: "God is light; in him there is *no darkness at all*" (1 John 1:5, emphasis added). I encourage readers to press through whatever cognitive dissonance they may be experiencing to seriously consider the perspective I propose.

While I contend that we must renounce the violence in this and every other sub-Christlike portrait of God, I have also indicated that I firmly believe we are not free to simply dismiss them. These portrayals are part of the God-breathed canon, and we must therefore trust that they hold a God-breathed, revelatory meaning—one that ultimately bears witness to Christ.

The revelatory meaning of these violent divine portraits is not found on the surface. It is, as Origen said, a buried treasure that requires effort to uncover. To discern it, we need to exercise the same surface-penetrating faith we exercise when we discern the full revelation of God in the sin-bearing crucified Christ—a figure who, on the surface, appears anything but divine. A figure who appears hideous, for he bears the ugly death consequences of our sin (Isaiah 52:14; 53:2–3).

Exploring the conquest narrative

We turn now to examine the genocidal portrait of Yahweh embedded in the conquest narrative through the lens of the cross.

The land that Israel came to possess—the promised land—is central to the biblical narrative. I see no reason to deny that God wanted his people to dwell there. Due to its geographical location, this land was ideally suited for Israel to fulfill Yahweh's original plan for them to become a blessing to the nations (Genesis 12:2–3; 15:18–21). However, the revelation of God in Christ gives us every reason to disbelieve that Yahweh wanted the Israelites to acquire this land by annihilating its indigenous population.

It's significant that the violent way the Israelites acquired this land—and the credit they gave to Yahweh for their violence—was entirely in line with how other ancient Near Eastern nations conquered land. In this context, taking possession of land meant slaughtering or enslaving its inhabitants. Furthermore, all nations attributed the violence they carried out to their gods, for ascribing such violence to a god was considered the highest form of praise.

Viewed in this light, I submit that when Yahweh communicated his desire for Israel to dwell in Canaan, Moses' fallen and culturally conditioned ears heard something akin to: "I want you to dwell in the land of Canaan, so you must slaughter the inhabitants of Canaan." This assumption would have been automatic for any ancient Near Eastern person. It explains why neither Joshua nor anyone else questioned or hesitated when Moses reported what he "heard" from Yahweh. As we've seen, people hear what they expect and are capable of hearing.

Since God works by means of influence rather than coercion, and since God had entered into a solemn covenant with his chosen people, God accommodated the fallen and culturally conditioned mindset of Moses, and of the Israelites. God meets people where they are, and this is where the Israelites were. This accommodation, however, meant that within the biblical narrative, God would take on the ugly appearance of a typical ancient Near Eastern warrior deity who commands and assists his people in mercilessly wiping out various populations.

Let's consider an alternate, cruciform, interpretation of the text. On Calvary, God stooped to bear our sin and thereby took on an appearance that reflected the ugliness of that sin. I submit that this is precisely what is going on behind the scenes of this genocide-commanding portrait of Yahweh along with every other sub-Christlike portrait in the inspired canon. The ugliness of this sin-reflecting divine portrait anticipates, and bears witness to, the ugliness of the sin-bearing cross. But if we view this portrait with the surface-penetrating eyes of a cross-informed faith, trusting that the God who stooped to become the crucified Christ has always been stooping out of love for his people, we will begin to discern this same beautiful, humble God in the depths of this ghastly portrait of the divine.

Viewed through our cross-informed faith, the canonical violent portraits of God become literary crucifixes. They bear witness to the truth that God has always been the sin-bearing, pouring-out God of radiant love who is fully revealed on the cross. These divine portraits are historic testimonies to the truth that "Jesus Christ is the same yesterday and today and forever" (Hebrews 13:8).

Confirming evidence

Once I adopted the cruciform hermeneutic, I was surprised to discover a wealth of biblical material I hadn't noticed before that confirmed it.[17] In the case of the conquest narrative, only after I had adopted this hermeneutic did I notice two passages in which Yahweh shared his plans about how he would have liked to relocate the the local people living there so his people could move in.

First, long before the Israelites violently invaded Canaan, Yahweh made this remarkable declaration: "I will send the hornet ahead of you to drive the Hivites, Canaanites and Hittites out of your way. But I will not drive them out in a single year, because the land would become desolate and the wild animals too numerous for you. Little by little, I will drive them out before you" (Exodus 23:28–30).

According to this passage, Yahweh's plan was to have the indigenous population of Canaan gradually migrate off the land by making it increasingly uncomfortable for them to remain. A swarm of pesky hornets might be annoying, but it's a far more gentle way of acquiring real estate than commanding your people to engage in full-scale genocide. So, we must wonder, what happened to this nonviolent plan?

The second passage is found in Leviticus 18:24–25, "Do not defile yourselves . . . because this is how the nations that I am going to drive out before you became defiled. Even the land was defiled; so I punished it for its sin, and the land vomited out its inhabitants."

Throughout Scripture, the welfare of land is directly tied to the spiritual state of its inhabitants. It seems Yahweh intended to allow the moral corruption of the Canaanites to render their land unfruitful, encouraging them to migrate to greener pastures naturally. No slaughtering would be necessary.

On top of this, there are a dozen other passages in which Yahweh says he will "drive out" the inhabitants of the areas he wanted for his children, without specifying how he would do this (e.g., Exodus 34:24; Deuteronomy 6:19; 11:23; Joshua 23:5). Yet none of these alternative, nonviolent plans were implemented. The inhabitants weren't driven out; they were enslaved or slaughtered.

How are we to explain the tremendous leap from God saying he will gradually relocate the indigenous population to Yahweh saying "show no mercy . . . completely destroy them" (Deuteronomy 7:1–2; 20:16–18)? Did God suddenly develop a foul mood? If we remain steadfast in our conviction the God looks like Jesus, this possibility can be quickly dismissed.

A more plausible explanation, I submit, is that Yahweh's nonviolent plans to take possession of the land were simply too radical for Moses, or anyone else, to grasp. Ancient Near Eastern people uniformly trusted in their gods to help them kill and acquire land, but no one ever dreamed of trusting in a god who would acquire a land on behalf of a people without needing them to kill anybody. And so, as happened when Jesus told his disciples about his impending suffering and death, Yahweh's nonviolent relocation plans fell on deaf ears. People hear what they expect and are capable of hearing.

Through the fresh perspective of a cross-informed faith, we can view these nonviolent plans as moments when the Spirit of Christ broke through to reveal how God truly wanted his people to inherit the land. And through this same lens, we can see the Spirit being suppressed by fallen cultural assumptions when Moses thought he heard Yahweh command, "Show no mercy . . . kill everything that breathes."

Whom are we going to trust?

When I claim that Moses heard what he expected to hear when he believed Yahweh commanded the Israelites to slaughter people, I do not mean to cast aspersions on him. Moses is one of the Bible's most esteemed heroes. However, like all biblical heroes—save one—Moses was not perfect, as the Pentateuch makes abundantly clear.[18] And, like the rest of us, one of his imperfections was that he was, to some degree, a product of his culture. This cultural conditioning inevitably influenced how Moses envisioned Yahweh, experienced Yahweh, and therefore how he heard from Yahweh. Unless we are diligently taking every thought captive to Christ (2 Corinthians 10:5), we are all susceptible to the same kind of influence.

It would be easy for us to judge Moses and other biblical heroes for the ruthless violence they carried out or commanded in God's name. Their violence must indeed be renounced. As I argued in the previous chapter, so long as Bible-trusting people embrace violent portraits of God, they will, to some degree, be less averse to violence than they otherwise would be. Yet, if we were in Moses' sandals, can any of us be certain we wouldn't have conceived of Yahweh or "heard" from Yahweh in the same twisted way?

While renouncing the violence of Moses' depiction of God, we must also look beyond it to appreciate his honest desire to know and love Yahweh, even with his distorted conception of him. I believe we also should honor the faithfulness and courage that Moses and other biblical heroes frequently displayed in their sincere attempts to follow Yahweh. As Vernard Eller insightfully notes, the only truth Moses and the ancient Israelites "missed" was "MAN IS NOT THE ENEMY." And we shouldn't fault them too much for this, Eller continues, for "it is not an easy truth to grasp," as evidenced by the fact that relatively few Christians throughout history have grasped it, despite the fact that this is explicitly taught in the New Testament (e.g., Ephesians 6:10–12, compare Matthew 5:44–45).[19]

Moses is to be honored, but I've been contending that, in light of who we know God to be in Christ, we cannot trust everything Moses says about God.

Another thing I never noticed until I began viewing Scripture through the lens of a cross-informed faith was that Moses is the only person who claimed to hear Yahweh utter the *herem* command. When Joshua later reiterated this command, he did so based on what "the LORD your God had commanded his servant Moses" (Joshua 9:24; compare 11:12, 20, 23). Given the ancient Near Eastern context, it's understandable that Joshua and the Israelites believed Moses. The question is, should we?

Consider Paul's words when he says, "Even if we or an angel from heaven should preach a gospel other than the one we preached to you, let them be under God's curse" (Galatians 1:8). Paul's gospel was "the message of the cross" (1 Corinthians 1:18), and it's hard to imagine a message more at odds with this gospel than Moses' message that Yahweh wanted his people to mercilessly slaughter people. "If we take Paul seriously, we shouldn't just question Moses' *herem* command—we should regard it as being "under a curse." This would hold true even if this command came from Paul himself or an angel from heaven!

If it seems hard to reconcile how God could "breathe" through something cursed, which implies estrangement from God, remember: this is precisely what God did on Calvary, when God breathed his full self-revelation through the man who bore our sin and our curse (Galatians 3:13).

My hope is that this chapter has helped you to experience what the woman in my congregation experienced. God wants all of us to experience the Spirit-inspired freedom to behold the glory of God in the face of Jesus Christ (2 Corinthians 3:17–18; 4:6) and to place our full trust in this revelation. And my hope is that readers are better equipped to find this same glory in all of Scripture's violent divine portraits. When viewed through a cross-centered faith, each becomes a literary crucifix that bears witness to the cross.

5

The Jesus-Looking Kingdom

Kingdom mission begins and ends with Jesus, the cruciform King.
—**SCOTT MCKNIGHT**, *KINGDOM CONSPIRACY*

It was the first day of class in my first semester at Yale Divinity School. At this point in my life, I identified as a conservative charismatic evangelical, and to be honest, I was a little nervous. My pastor and most of my evangelical Christian friends disapproved of my decision to attend YDS. They warned me that this "bastion of liberalism," as one friend called it, would corrupt my faith and turn me into one of "them." Despite their dire predictions and heartfelt pleas to reconsider, I stubbornly left my church and friends in 1979 to study at YDS.

And so, there I was—on the first day of class—surrounded by "liberals" (or so I assumed). After introducing himself and outlining the course, the professor picked up a piece of chalk and wrote a single question on the blackboard: "What is the kingdom of God?" He then instructed us to break into groups of four or five, introduce ourselves, and take turns sharing what we thought the kingdom of God meant.

I'm embarrassed to admit that, at this stage in my spiritual journey, the only thing that came to mind when I thought about the kingdom of God was the rapture and going to heaven. But as I listened to the other three people in my group share their views rooted far more in this world—answers like "social justice," "no racism or sexism," and "world peace"—I quickly realized my other-worldly answer wouldn't fly. So, I drew from my college experience working at a group home for children with intellectual disabilities and offered, "the disabled are cared for." My answer was warmly received.

Things became interesting when the professor wheeled out a large white drawing board. He invited volunteers from each group to come forward, one by one, to draw a symbolic representation of an idea their group felt captured the essence of the kingdom of God. The first half-dozen volunteers went smoothly and predictably.

Then, a female student stepped up, drew the earth encased in a heart, and confidently proclaimed, "The kingdom of God is when all are cared for, regardless of what they're able to contribute." Next, a bold young man drew a surprisingly detailed farmer riding on a tractor and declared, "In the kingdom of God, everyone will take responsibility and do their fair share—no freeloaders!"

A subtle ripple of tension moved through the room, but I silently exhaled in relief. "I'm not the only conservative in this school!" I thought.

What happened next, however, sent the tension skyrocketing. Another student approached the board and drew a woman holding a baby. With equal boldness, she proclaimed, "The kingdom of God is where all babies are wanted babies!" Instantly, another young man shot up from his chair and stormed toward the board with a fierce expression. The room grew palpably tense. Before he could grab the marker, however, the professor mercifully called time and declared the project over.

To this day, I've wondered what that young man was planning to draw.

The professor's question, What is the kingdom of God? was incredibly important—and not just for that day. It's a question we all must wrestle with, as the central message of Jesus is "The kingdom of God has come near" (see Luke 10:9–10). Yet, as my classroom experience demonstrated, without a shared understanding, people tend to project their highest values onto the kingdom. Whatever they consider good and just becomes their version of the kingdom. But as the incident in class also revealed—and as is painfully evident in America today—people often disagree about what "good" and "just" actually mean, especially when it comes to complex social and political issues.

This is not a new problem. Throughout church history, people have tended to define the kingdom of God according to their own intuitions and ideals. While I assume their intentions were usually sincere, we can all agree that some interpretations were profoundly misguided. Consider, for example, the sixteenth-century Spanish conquistadors. They subjugated, enslaved, and massacred Indigenous populations, all while sincerely believing they were advancing God's kingdom. Looking back, it's clear they were simply conflating the kingdom with the political and nationalistic agendas of their earthly empires. Indeed, whenever Christians have taken up arms in the name of the kingdom, it has always been political and nationalistic interests driving them, cloaked, of course, in kingdom language.

If we want to understand the true nature of God's kingdom, we cannot assume it aligns with our fallen intuitions or culturally conditioned assumptions about what is good and just. Instead, we must fix our eyes on Jesus. Only then can we see the kingdom of God for what it truly is.

The kingdom is all about love

True to form, Scripture doesn't provide us with an abstract definition of the kingdom of God; instead, it offers us a story. And this story centers entirely on the person of Jesus Christ.

Throughout the Gospels, Jesus is depicted as the perfect embodiment—the incarnation—of the kingdom of God. Put another way, Jesus' life was a "dome" over which God reigned as King. Jesus' complete surrender to the Father and the Spirit enabled him to proclaim "the kingdom of God is near" to whomever he was present. According to the New Testament, Jesus inaugurated this kingdom through his ministry, death, and resurrection. He then entrusted the church—the community of all who submit to his lordship—with the task of embodying, living out, and expanding this kingdom.[1]

When this kingdom is lived out, individually and collectively, it always looks like Jesus. God looks like Jesus, and when God's people embody God's reign, this too looks like Jesus. This is why the New Testament emphasizes the necessity of imitating Christ. As Paul instructs: "Be imitators of God," (NRSVue), which means that we are to "Walk in the way of love, just as Christ loved us and gave himself up for us" (Ephesians 5:1–2).

Consider the weight of this call. We are summoned to do nothing less than imitate *God*. This is the very essence of being "godly" or God-like. The Greek word for "imitate" (*mimetes*) conveys the idea of mimicking or shadowing someone. As Jesus' shadow, we are to replicate what we have seen God do in him. We are to love as Christ loved us on the cross—nothing more (for that would be impossible) and nothing less.

Living in Christlike love is the beginning, middle, and end of everything we are called to do. Both Paul and Peter emphasize the supremacy of love when they write, "Above all, clothe yourselves with love" (Colossians 3:14 NRSVue; 1 Peter 4:8). Above all! Love is to be worn like a garment, shaping every thought, word, and action. Cross-shaped love must characterize everything we do. As Paul exhorts elsewhere: "Let all that you do be done in love" (1 Corinthians 16:14 NRSVue). There is never a time, with anyone, in any situation, for any reason, where we are permitted to act outside of Christlike love.

Think about this the next time you're in an argument, get cut off by a reckless driver, or hear an insurance agent tell you the medical procedure your child needs is not covered. Christlike love must govern our response in all circumstances.

Paul presses even further in 1 Corinthians 13, declaring that anything done without love is utterly worthless:

- You may possess the most eloquent gift of tongues in heaven and on earth, but without love, it is nothing more than an irritating noise (v. 1).

- You may have "all knowledge" and understand "all mysteries," but without love, your insight has no kingdom value (v. 2).

- You may have faith that can move mountains or perform every imaginable good work, but if we're motivated by anything other than cruciform love, it is all utterly worthless (v. 2).

- You may give away all you "possess to the poor" and endure great "hardship" to help others, but if it's done to look good instead of expressing love, you "gain nothing" (v. 3).

The singular criterion for assessing the kingdom value of anything we say or do is love. As Paul states, "The only thing that counts is faith working through love" (Galatians 5:6 NRSVue). If we miss this, we have missed everything.

The fastest-growing churches, the most celebrated preachers, the most inspiring worship services, the most impressive display of spiritual gifts, the most acclaimed scholarship—all of these are nothing but religious noise to God unless they reflect the love displayed on the cross.

When God reigns over a community, you'll find people growing in Christlike, cruciform love. In such a community, people grow in their capacity to refrain from retaliation, choosing instead to overcome evil with good (Matthew 5:39; Romans 12:17–21). You'll find them cultivating a gentle and humble spirit (Ephesians 4:2; Titus 3:2; 1 Peter 3:4, 8), putting others' interests ahead of their own (Philippians 2:4; 1 Corinthians 10:24, 33), and carrying one another's burdens (Ephesians 4:2). You'll find them going beyond what is asked of them (Matthew 5:40–42) and washing the feet of others, even those who betray them (John 13:14–15).

The kingdom is displayed when people feed the hungry, clothe the naked, shelter the homeless, befriend the friendless, and visit condemned prisoners (James 2:15–17; 1 John 3:14–18; compare Matthew 25:34–40). God's reign is present wherever people are learning to love unconditionally and indiscriminately, just as our heavenly Father loves (Matthew 5:39–45; Luke 6:27–36).

This is what the kingdom of God looks like—because this is what Jesus looks like, and, therefore, this is what God looks like.

Serving Muslim refugees

One of the most spectacular illustrations of the kingdom I've ever witnessed happened while I was on a teaching tour in Scotland several years ago. I was invited to a Friday evening church service at the Upper Room in Glasgow, held in the home of Cindy and Wes White, the lead pastors of the most unusual congregation I've ever encountered. The modest house was packed with over fifty people, and to my great surprise, the vast majority were Muslim Iranian refugees. As we mingled over snacks before the service began, I learned that some of these Muslims had become followers of Jesus, while others had not. Yet, there was no trace of awkwardness or judgment over anyone's faith.

At one point, I asked a young Iranian man who was enthusiastically enjoying a pastry if he was a Muslim or a follower of Jesus. Smiling with his mouth half-full, he replied, "I worship Allah, but I deeply appreciate what you Christians are doing for us." After a sip of Pepsi, he added, "But I'm considering becoming a Christian. My friend, who came with me to Scotland, converted a few weeks ago and is trying to persuade me to join him." He then shrugged his shoulders playfully and said, "Who knows?"

When it was time, Wes invited everyone into the cramped living room. A guitarist led us in several worship songs, and to my amazement, many of the Muslims joined in, even when praising Jesus! It was as strange as it was beautiful.

Then Wes introduced a young Iranian woman and called on her to sit in "the prayer chair," explaining that this woman's immigration court date was approaching. Christians as well as Muslims then gathered around her to pray. Some prayed in English, others in Farsi. Some prayed to Jesus, others to Allah. The room was saturated with the tangible presence of God's Spirit and the warmth of God's love. I was moved to tears, having never before witnessed Christians and Muslims praying together.

Afterward, Wes invited anyone curious about Jesus to stay for a teaching, which six attenders did.

This is what a typical church service looks like at the Upper Room.

I later learned that this "prayer chair" was central to how this kingdom community began. Two years earlier, Wes and Cindy, along with another two couples, felt called to establish a kingdom community in the Glasgow area. They started by asking the all-important kingdom questions: How can we serve people? What needs can we help meet?[2]

They soon discovered a community of Iranian refugees in their area struggling to navigate Scotland's asylum process. It turns out it is relatively easy to enter Scotland, but rather difficult to be granted asylum and follow a path toward citizenship. One of the members of Wes' and Cindy's team had some legal training, so this team began to help refugees prepare for their court appearance and to accompany them to it. The person being helped, and whoever wanted to join them, would be invited to Wes' and Cindy's house on a Friday night to discuss their case and to pray for them, and this is how the "prayer chair" came about.

Typically, only around 25 percent of refugees who apply for asylum in Scotland are granted it. But over the previous two years, nearly every refugee represented by this team won their case. Word spread quickly among the Iranian refugees about these court-savvy, compassionate Christians. The Friday gatherings grew, fostering fellowship, prayer, and eventually some conversions. By the time I visited, over sixty individuals or families represented by Wes's team had been granted asylum, and about half of them had surrendered their lives to Christ. On top of this, two of these new converts decided to risk imprisonment by returning to Iran as missionaries.

Where God's kingdom is present, humble love strives to meet people's needs. Desperate lives find hope. Dividing walls of culture and religion fall. And people are loved into God's reign, where they joyfully surrender their lives to Christ.

The crisis in the church

God has staked everything on the church loving this way. Jesus declared, "By this everyone will know that you are my disciples, if you love one another" (John 13:35). In his prayer in

John 17, Jesus asked that his disciples embody the perfect love of the Trinity so that the world would know he had been sent by the Father (see vv. 22– vv. 22– 23). This phrase "so that" highlights the divine strategy. The church is to be known for its radical, scandalous love—a love so extraordinary that it raises questions that only appealing to the reality of Jesus can answer.

Does this Jesus-emulating, cross-shaped love characterize the church today? Which is to ask, does the church today reflect the presence of the kingdom of God? Does the church resemble the crucified Christ by pouring itself out on behalf of others, including its enemies?

The answer is as tragic as it is obvious. Thank God for the magnificent expressions of the Jesus-looking kingdom, such as the Upper Room, that are springing up all around the globe. While church attendance in Western countries continues to decline, the Spirit has been working to birth a movement of people around the globe who understand that God looks like Jesus and that our call is to look like Jesus and to change the world in a Jesus kind of way—not by acquiring political power to force change, but by embodying the humble, other-oriented love of God.[3]

Yet, if Christlike love is the benchmark for the spiritual health of churches, it seems the church in the West, and in America in particular, is wildly missing the mark. Studies have consistently found that the majority of non-Christian young Americans view Christians as narrow-minded, judgmental, hypocritical, and anti-LGBTQ.[4] This is the worst news possible for the body that is called to be known by its scandalous love, as Jesus was.

In light of the absolute priority given to love in the New Testament, I frankly think we'd be better off disbelieving the Trinity, or the incarnation, or any other doctrine, for to miss the mark on our call to imitate Jesus by living in love is to miss *everything*.

Keeping the kingdom holy

Jesus taught us to pray: "Our Father in heaven, hallowed be your name, your kingdom come, your will be done, on earth as it is in heaven" (Matthew 6:9–10).

At the heart of this prayer is a petition for the Father's name to be hallowed. In Scripture, the Father's name signifies his character and reputation, while the word "hallowed" means to keep it holy, set apart, and distinct from everything else. Significantly, this is the prayer's opening petition, underscoring that only by keeping the Father's name completely set apart from everything else can we fulfill his holy will and embody his holy kingdom "on earth as it is in heaven."

This has always been the church's greatest challenge, however—and far too often, its greatest failing. Instead of keeping the Father's name distinct and advancing a kingdom that is radically different from all others, the church has frequently allowed culture and politics to redefine "God's kingdom," as my first class at Yale Divinity School illustrated.

Jacques Ellul captures this tragedy with piercing clarity; Christianity, he observes, has often functioned like "an empty bottle that successive cultures fill in with all kinds of things." And he continues: "Under a monarchy, Christianity became monarchist; under a republic, it became republican; under socialism, it became socialist." In this regard," Ellul concludes, "Christianity is the opposite of what we are shown by the revelation of God in Jesus Christ."[5]

This dynamic has played out repeatedly throughout history. Whenever the church has lost its Jesus-centered vision of the kingdom, a void is created—a void that is inevitably filled with cultural, political, and nationalistic ideals. Instead of offering the world an alternative kingdom, the church became the religious wing of whatever earthly kingdom it found herself embedded in. The church has always preached salvation through Christ, but its fundamental mission often devolved into merely asking God to bless the earthly kingdom it was embedded in to bring it prosperity and military victories.

When Pilate asked Jesus if he was the "King of the Jews," Jesus replied: "My kingdom is not of this world. If it were, my servants would fight to prevent my arrest by the Jewish leaders. But now my kingdom is from another place" (John 18:36).

Jesus' statement is a defining declaration of his kingdom's nature. His kingdom is "not of this world," as evidenced by the fact that his followers did not take up arms to defend their King. The contrast between God's kingdom and all earthly kingdoms could not be starker:

- Earthly kingdoms rely on human rulers, but in God's kingdom, we place our trust solely in God. To trust in a human king—or president—is to reject God as our true King (1 Samuel 8:7).

- Earthly kingdoms resort to violence when deemed necessary, but in God's kingdom, violence toward enemies is replaced by love for enemies.

- Earthly kingdoms operate through power over others, enforced by laws and threats. God's kingdom, by contrast, operates through power under others—the humble, servant-like, self-sacrificial love of Christ.

- Earthly kingdoms seek to regulate behavior, but God's kingdom seeks to transform hearts, conforming people to the image of Christ—a transformation that laws and threats can never accomplish.

If you live in a democratic nation like America, you are periodically asked to express your opinions by voting, thus deciding how the country should be run and who should run it. This is all well and good; follow your conscience at the polls. But it is absolutely crucial we do not confuse our political opinions with our kingdom convictions. God's kingdom is not a "new and improved" version of the kingdoms of this world. It is something altogether different. And preserving this difference—keeping the Father's name holy—is of utmost importance.

Whenever this distinction is blurred, whether by conforming to the dominant culture or by mistaking political allegiances for kingdom convictions, the unique beauty of God's indiscriminate, cross-centered love is lost. And when this love is obscured, our sacred call to embody it in the world is compromised.

Be the change you want to see

I'd like to close this chapter by giving three words of advice about living out the kingdom.

Start with yourself. I imagine some might be thinking, "The church needs to repent!" And indeed, I believe large swaths of it do need to repent. But while the church is a collective whole, it is comprised of individuals, and only individuals can choose to repent. And the only individual you have any control over, and thus the only individual you can bring to repentance, is *yourself.*

Before we cast accusatory fingers for the world's problems at an institution, be it the church, a political party, modern society, greedy corporate executives, or anything else, we should first look in the mirror. Gandhi spoke a piece of kingdom wisdom when he famously said, "Be the change you want to see in the world."

If you want to see more love in the church and more love in the world, commit to "walking in the way of love" twenty-four seven. As you go about your day, cultivate the habit of agreeing with God that every person you encounter has unsurpassable worth, as evidenced by the fact that God was willing to pay an unsurpassable price for them, and whisper a private blessing over them. And if the occasion presents itself, express your agreement with God by helping the person out any way you can. It's a tiny act of love that only takes a couple of seconds, but it's the many little decisions we make, or don't make, in our day-to-day lives that form our character, for better or for worse, and that advance the kingdom.

Find a community. The kingdom is not comprised of individuals striving to live in Christlike love on their own. Jesus and the New Testament speak of the kingdom as a community. Every one of the fifty-seven "one anothers" we find recorded in the New Testament assume that Jesus followers are sharing life together.[6] We are members of one "body," and you know how much good a member of your physical body is if it gets detached from the rest of your body (1 Corinthians 12:7–27).

The call to live an other-oriented life is a call to swim upstream against the strong current of our individualistic, consumeristic, and increasingly self-focused culture. It's highly unlikely you can do this on your own, and by God's own design, you aren't supposed to try to do this on your own. If you are serious about being conformed to the image of Jesus instead of the image of a typical American consumer, you are going to need to find a community that is also aspiring to live like Christ. Swimming upstream is not easy!

Pray for your enemies. We've seen that Jesus stipulated that loving our enemies and doing good to those who oppose us was the benchmark for being considered a child of the Father, for this is how the Father loves (Matthew 5:44-45; Luke 6:27–35). Nothing is more countercultural in Jesus' teaching than this instruction.

Whenever I share Jesus or Paul's teaching on loving enemies and refraining from violence, I often hear the response, "So, if someone breaks into your home and is going to rape your wife, you're saying Jesus expects us to do nothing?" I first explain that when Jesus says, "Do not resist an evildoer," the word for "resist" (*antistemi*) implies resisting force with force.

Jesus is instructing us to not respond to violence with violence, but he's not telling us to respond by doing nothing.

To help guide our response to an evildoer, I encourage people to imagine the evildoer is a loved one—a son or daughter, a sibling, a friend. If this loved one went crazy and suddenly broke into your home with the intent of harming someone, you'd do everything in your power to stop them, but you'd cause as little harm as possible, and you certainly would not kill them. And the reason is because, as much as you love those you want to protect, you would also love your beloved aggressor.

This is the attitude Jesus is teaching us to cultivate. When he instructs his hearers to "love your enemies," he's not saying to "refrain from violence even though you hate your enemy." He's rather saying, "Learn how to genuinely love your enemy." Cultivate the kind of character that would genuinely care about the well-being of an aggressor, and that would therefore respond to the aggressor in ways that are consistent with love.

The thing is, we never achieve proficiency at anything without practice. A person can't expect to hit a home run in the bottom of the ninth if they haven't put in time practicing their swing. So too, we can't expect to be able to love threatening evildoers if we haven't spent time exercising that muscle. And, as I've said, this is the most important muscle for us to get in shape.

To this end, I want to encourage readers to pick out the top three to five people or groups they have the hardest time loving, and commit to praying for them every day. Agree with God that this person or group was worth Jesus dying for and pray blessings on them. It may be very hard at first, but I encourage you to be persistent. And watch what God will do *in you* if you are persistent.

You will find, in time, that your anger toward this person or group is slowly replaced with compassion. And you may, in time, begin to see what God sees in this person or group—something more profound than all the things you don't like about them. You may come to see the unsurpassable worth of this "enemy," and now you're beginning to love this "enemy" the way Christ loved you, and gave his life for you, even while you were an enemy of God (Romans 5:8).

The character of God's kingdom reflects the character of God as revealed in Jesus. Thus, God's kingdom is a Jesus-looking kingdom. But how does understanding God's character through the lens of Jesus influence our view of other divine attributes traditionally ascribed to God, such as "immutability" and "impassibility"? This is the question we will explore in the next chapter.

6

Rethinking God

God is not inscrutable—there is nothing beyond or behind what we see in Christ.

—REINHARD FELDERMEIER AND **HERMAN SPIECKERMAN**, *GOD OF THE LIVING*

You know the scene: Dorothy, Toto, the Tin Man, the Scarecrow, and the cowardly Lion stand before the mighty Oz, who appears as a terrifying giant head before them and speaks with a loud and angry-sounding voice. The five travelers are petrified until little Toto pulls back a curtain and exposes the ruse. The real Oz, it turns out, is just an ordinary guy speaking into a microphone and pulling levers to create the frightening image. And once Dorothy and her friends discover the truth, they were no longer afraid of the terrifying illusion the wizard of Oz had created.

Sometimes the frightening way someone appears differs from the truth, and when the truth is discovered, the frightening appearance loses its power. It can work in the opposite direction as well. Sometimes, the loving way someone appears differs from the truth, and when the truth is discovered, the loving appearance loses its power.

Christian theologians have often struggled with the problem of appearances conflicting with reality. As I mentioned in chapter 1, theologians have frequently distinguished between God as he appears in Christ and God as he is in himself. While all Christian theologians have held that God is revealed in Christ, the dominant theological tradition of the church—known as "classical theism"—has ascribed to God attributes that seem to contradict this revelation. And as with Dorothy and her friends, if one accepts that the truth of who God is apart from revelation is quite different from the way God appears in his revelation in Christ, it can change how they think about, and respond to, the revelation of God in Christ.

In what follows, I will review and critique classical theism before moving on to discuss the way the cross should transform our understanding of other divine attributes as well as our understanding of God's response to evil and suffering.

The classical view of God

The classical view of God has been embraced in various forms by many of the church's most influential theologians, from Augustine to Thomas Aquinas to the Protestant Reformers. At its core, classical theism rests on several key metaphysical assumptions that originate in ancient Greek philosophy, three of which are worth examining.[1]

Classical assumption #1: Anything with the potential to change is imperfect. In the words of Aquinas, God is "absolutely actuality . . . with no potentiality at all."[2] Therefore, God is altogether immutable and cannot change. This assumption leads to the belief that, while God is the primary cause of all that exists, nothing that exists produces any change in God. Even God's knowledge of us, according to this view, is not dependent on us, because that would imply we bring about change in God. Instead, God knows us only by knowing Godself as our primary cause. For this reason, Aquinas logically concluded that "being related to God is a reality in creatures, but . . . not a reality to God."[3] As Thomist scholar Herbert McCabe put it, "creation adds nothing to God." Hence, "all the difference it makes is . . . to the creatures."[4]

This assumption faces serious challenges. For one, it implies theological determinism, undermining human free will and making God the ultimate author of evil. Moreover, it undermines the authenticity of our relationship with God. How can we relate to a deity who is entirely unaffected by us? In fact, if God is the ultimate cause of everything we think and do, it is hard to see how there is a distinct "us" for God to relate to.

But the most fundamental problem with this assumption is that it contradicts the revelation of God in Christ. If we begin with Jesus instead of abstract metaphysical premises, I don't see how it would ever occur to anyone to think of God as incapable of change. Jesus is the Word made flesh (John 1:14), which means the eternal Word transitioned *from* a state of not being human *to* a state of being human. This transition presupposes that the Word had the potential for change.

A Jesus-centered view of God affirms that God does not change *in character*, for "Jesus Christ is the same yesterday and today and forever" (Hebrews 13:8). Yet as a loving, relational being, God is responsive—capable of changing in response to what happens in our lives. Scripture testifies to this dynamic responsiveness repeatedly. For example, in Jeremiah we learn that whenever Yahweh declares that judgment is coming on a nation, he is willing to "change his mind" and bless that nation if it repents (e.g., Jeremiah 18:1–10 ISV). This is a God we *can* truly relate to—a God who is capable of being moved by, and changed through, his relationship with us.

Classical assumption #2: Everything in time changes and is thus imperfect. Therefore, God exists in a timeless, eternal present.
This assumption also raises significant relational difficulties.

Relationships require reciprocity—I affect you, and you affect me. But this mutual interaction presupposes that both participants exist within the flow of time.

If we start with Jesus, the idea of a timeless God becomes hard to sustain. Again, the Word *became* flesh—a statement that presupposes God experiences a "before" (pre-incarnation) and "after" (post-incarnation). Similarly, the one who said, "Anyone who has seen me has seen the Father" (John 14:9) spent his entire ministry responding to peoples' needs. Jesus thus reveals that the Father is moved by the plight of people, which refutes the classical idea of God existing in an eternally unchanging present moment.

Certainly, God's experience of time differs from ours: "With the Lord a day is like a thousand years, and a thousand years are like a day" (2 Peter 3:8). But if God looks like Jesus, we cannot avoid the conclusion that God's experience involves a "before" and "after." Every verb applied to Jesus—and to God throughout the Bible—presupposes this. While it is difficult to imagine having a relationship with a tenseless deity, relating to a Jesus-looking God who shares our experience of time poses no such problem.

Classical assumption #3: Passions and vulnerability to suffering indicate weakness and imperfection. Therefore, God is devoid of passions and cannot suffer ("impassible"). If we start with Jesus, I do not see how it is possible to come to believe that God is devoid of passion or incapable of suffering. Jesus experienced profound anguish. As he faced crucifixion, he sweated blood under the weight of his grief. Most significantly, on the cross, Jesus endured the unimaginable agony of bearing the sin of the world and the experience of alienation from God that comes with it. This is why he cried out, "My God, my God, why have you forsaken me?" (Matthew 27:46).

While the Father never abandoned Jesus, the Son experienced the God-alienating curse of sin that he bore on our behalf. If we deny that God can suffer, however, what does Jesus' suffering reveal? This question is crucial because the depth of Jesus' suffering demonstrates the depth of God's love for us—a love that eternally defines God's triune fellowship. But if Jesus suffered only in his humanity and not in his divinity, as classical theists claim, then the cross reveals nothing significant about God.

Unnecessary mysteries

The shortcomings of classical theism stem from its starting point: a philosophical conception of God that is then forced to fit the revelation of God in Christ. Classical theologians have gone to great lengths attempting to reconcile the classical view of God with the dynamic, interactive God fully revealed in Christ and that is reflected throughout the biblical narrative. All such attempts generate a number of apparent contradictions that classical theologians smooth over by calling them "mysteries."

God is immutable, but in some mysterious sense also is relational. God is timeless, but in some mysterious way also interactive. God is impassible, but in some mysterious manner, also suffers.

Are these legitimate "mysteries," or are they simply contradictions? I believe the latter. But my more fundamental critique is that these contradictions arise only because classical theists begin with reason-based metaphysical assumptions about God. This approach yields a conception of God that mirrors ancient Greek philosophical ideas, such as Aristotle's "unmoved mover."[5] Unlike Aristotle, however, Christian theologians were obliged to in some mysterious sense also affirm the biblical portrayal of God as personal and relational.

While reason certainly has its place in understanding God, it should not be our starting point. Instead, we must begin with Jesus Christ, trusting that nothing about God contradicts what Jesus reveals. When we start here, the "mysteries" of classical theism simply disappear.

Rethinking God's transcendence and wisdom

Once we establish that Jesus is the full revelation of God's very essence (Hebrews 1:3), every other aspect of God takes on new meaning. In the remainder of this chapter, I'll briefly examine God's transcendence and wisdom from a cross-centered perspective before concluding with a cruciform understanding of the problem of evil.

To begin, let me clarify: my critique of the so-called mysteries of classical theism should not be taken as a denial of legitimate mysteries surrounding God. There most certainly are legitimate mysteries, but unlike the unnecessary mysteries I've critiqued, the legitimate mysteries of God involve paradoxes that surpass human understanding without lapsing into logical contradictions.

Consider the traditional concept of God's transcendence, which affirms that God is "wholly other" than creation. While all created things are finite in time and space, God has no spatial or temporal limits (which, as I've argued, does not entail that God has no "before" or "after"). While we cannot fully conceive of such a being, there is no contradiction in affirming this mystery.

Similarly, created things are dependent on other things for their existence, but God's existence depends on nothing. This self-existence, or "aseity," as theologians call it, is likewise a mystery that defies our comprehension, but it does not involve a logical contradiction. The same holds true for every other aspect of God's eternal being that is "wholly other" than creation.

I accept these traditional affirmations and the mystery they point to for both biblical and philosophical reasons. But in my view, they do not go far enough. What is often left out of these formulations is the recognition that God's "wholly other" essential being is most fully revealed on the cross.

In Revelation 5, John envisions the slain Lamb—the crucified and resurrected Christ—"standing at the center of the throne" (Revelation 5:6). This throne belongs to the indescribable, transcendent God, whom John portrays with awe-inspiring imagery: "the appearance of jasper and ruby," encircled by "a rainbow that shone like an emerald" (Revelation 4:3). Taken literally, this imagery becomes nonsensical. How can the Lamb stand on the very throne where the transcendent God is sitting? But when we let the symbolism speak on its own terms, a profound truth emerges: the slain Lamb embodies the very heart of the transcendent God. The cross is not simply a momentary expression of God's character—it is the ultimate revelation of God's eternal essence.

As Paul declares, "all the treasures of wisdom and knowledge" are hidden in Christ (Colossians 2:3). Since Paul's claim is all-encompassing, we should look not only to the way God contrasts with creation to discern God's transcendence; we must first look in the event where God came closest to us: the cross, where God fully identified with our sin and our curse.

Could anything better reflect the unfathomable, transcendent nature of God than the moment when the all-holy God stooped to experience the sin of the world? Or when the God whose very essence is perfect, loving unity endured the alienation from God that sin carries with it? Could anything better demonstrate the "wholly other" nature of God than the cross, where God displayed God's omnipotent strength by becoming weak and God's infinite wisdom by appearing foolish? Could anything be more beautifully mysterious than this?

Jesus' shocking teachings and life culminate in his even more shocking crucifixion. Through it all, he reveals a God whose love astonishes us precisely because it transcends everything humanity has ever dreamed God—or the gods—could be.

Cruciform wisdom

Christians have always affirmed that God is omniscient, meaning that God knows everything. Theologians may debate the implications of this, but all agree on its basic definition. However, instead of merely affirming the all-encompassing scope of what God knows, I believe, in light of the cross, that it is even more vital to affirm the all-encompassing scope of God's wisdom. God's wisdom is about not only what God knows, but more importantly, what God *does* with all that God knows.

Where do we look to understand this divine wisdom? Unsurprisingly, the New Testament points us to the cross. As we have seen, Paul *identifies* the cross as "the power of God" (1 Corinthians 1:18). He calls the crucified Christ the wisdom that God kept "hidden" as a "mystery" through the ages (1 Corinthians 2:7; Colossians 1:26–27). This wisdom, Paul explains, was something the "rulers [*archonton*] of this age" failed to grasp—"for if they had, they would not have crucified the Lord of glory" (1 Corinthians 2:8).

These "rulers" influenced wicked people to crucify Jesus, a point confirmed in the Gospels (John 13:27). However, the powers unwittingly played into God's wise plan. Oblivious to the wise plan that was in play, these principalities and powers had no clue why Jesus had come to earth. Hence, demons recognized Jesus as the Son of God but could only make wild guesses as to his mission (e.g., Matthew 8:29; Mark 1:24). What they apparently *did* understand, however, was that if the Word had become human, he was killable. And so they carried out their diabolic scheme, only to watch the whole thing backfire.

As Paul explains, Jesus' death canceled "the charge of our legal indebtedness" that had held us in bondage. In this way, God disarmed the "powers and authorities" (Colossians 2:14–15). So, these powers orchestrated the crucifixion, yet this very act led to their undoing, making them a "public spectacle"—a divine irony that highlights God's wisdom.

This demonstrates the heart of God's wisdom. By exploiting the powers' self-induced inability to understand love, God used their diabolical schemes to bring about their own implosion. We might say that, because of their self-induced blindness, "the rulers of this age" foolishly brought a Trojan horse into their own camp when they crucified Christ (1 Corinthians 2:8). For on the cross, the light of God's love shone in the darkness, and the darkness could not overcome it (John 1:5).

God is all-knowing and all-wise, and what Jesus' self-sacrificial death reveals is that God is always wisely eradicating evil and establishing his shalom throughout the cosmos by means of the blood of the cross (Colossians 1:19–20). And it is this wisdom, and this love, that the church is called to participate in, to proclaim, and to place its ultimate hope in.

The wisdom of the slain Lamb may appear "foolish" and "weak" by the world's standards, but it is the only wisdom capable of defeating evil permanently. And this is why our ultimate hope must not be in the wisdom of political parties, or in the wisdom of our nation, or in technology. Our hope is in the One who, with infinite wisdom, "made known to us the mystery of his will according to his good pleasure, which he purposed in Christ . . . to bring unity to all things in heaven and on earth under Christ" (Ephesians 1:9–10).

The cruciform problem of evil

Finally, if we anchor our thinking about God in the cross, it transforms how we understand the problem of evil. As I've noted, a cross-centered understanding of divine power reveals that God's power is the influential power of love—not a coercive power that overrides free will. God creates us as free agents out of love, inviting us to participate in his love while always respecting our personhood. The same applies to the innumerable agents that populate "the heavenly realms" (Ephesians 6:12).

The risk God took in creating free agents is that they might choose paths contrary to his will, paths that are destructive to themselves and to all under their influence. This, I contend, is the most fundamental answer to the problem of evil. It's called the "free will defense." It comes down to this: Either evil originates in God's will, or it originates in wills other than God's. If we believe that "God is light, and in him there is no darkness at all" (1 John 1:5), then, so far as I can see, we have no choice but to ascribe evil to these other wills, both human and angelic.

However, the cross reveals a deeper dimension to the problem of evil. The crucifixion shows us a God who makes evil his own problem. The God who reveals himself in Jesus does not stand aloof from the pain of the world; instead, he enters into the depths of our collective hell to liberate creation from it. If evil is a problem for us, how much more must it be for a God whose capacity for love is infinite and who therefore experiences the world's collective pain?

This means that God is present within your pain, sharing it with you. I, for one, have found immense comfort in this truth.

"I thirst"

Two years ago, I lay on a couch in the emergency room, sweating, shaking, and dying of thirst. I was later diagnosed with a super-bug infection, likely acquired during a previous emergency department visit the week before for a kidney stone and infection. It had been a rough couple of weeks!

The emergency department was packed, and I had to wait for hours without being allowed to drink water. I'd never felt such intense thirst or misery in my life.

As I lay there, I decided to pray for others in the room, knowing that acts of service are the best antidote to misery.

RETHINKING GOD · 115

Suddenly, a vivid image of Jesus on the cross appeared in my mind. His face was bloodied and etched with unimaginable pain. Then, he raised his head, looked at me with eyes full of compassion, and said, "I thirst."

I began to weep. Jesus was telling me he was sharing my suffering. My physical discomfort didn't diminish, but my soul soared. By sharing in Christ's suffering, I entered more deeply into his pain, deepening my love for him and my sense of his love for me. I was witnessing God wisely bringing some redemptive good out of my miserable situation (Romans 8:28).

Whether it's physical, psychological, emotional, or spiritual pain you're carrying, invite the One who is the wisdom of God on the inside to experience it with you, and experience the difference this makes.

If we center the cross in all our thinking, as I believe we must, it compels us to rethink everything we once believed about God. Many aspects of the traditional Christian understanding of God can and should be retained, but others cannot—such as the classical notions of God being completely changeless, existing in a single eternal unchanging moment, and being incapable of passions and suffering. Still other aspects need to be expanded or reimagined, as I have argued in the case of God's transcendence, God's wisdom, and the free will defense of the problem of evil.

A final word must be said on the basis of the cross, and for many it may be the most important word. It concerns the blessed hope that the crucified and risen Christ offers us.

7

The Blessed Hope

*We must accept finite disappointment,
but never lose infinite hope.*
—**MARTIN LUTHER KING JR.**

Thanks in part to Hal Lindsey's bestselling book *The Late Great Planet Earth*, an apocalyptic fervor gripped the hearts of multitudes of conservative churches in the 1970s, including the Pentecostal church I converted to in 1974. One of the first things I was taught as a new believer was that Jesus was going to return at any moment, because, I was told, the book of Revelation predicted things that were coming to pass in our day. And when Jesus returns, I was told, Christians will be "raptured" just before the world goes to hell in a handbasket.

For a while it was exhilarating expecting to get suctioned into the sky at any moment, but I found it difficult to sustain. On top of this, it wasn't long before I learned that our crystal ball way of reading Revelation was wrongheaded and that the rapture doctrine was unheard of in church history up until the early nineteenth century.[1] Nor was it long before I came to view the rapture doctrine as harmful since it encourages an escapist mindset and a dismissive attitude toward the problems of our world. Since I associated Jesus' second coming with this wrongheaded and escapist mindset, I have had little interest in Jesus' return throughout most of my life.

Only recently have I been forced to face the fact that my dismissive attitude toward Jesus' end-of-the-age appearance is radically at odds with the New Testament.[2] Indeed, only in the last few years have I come to understand how important is the conviction that God looks like Jesus to remaining hopeful, especially when it feels like the world is coming undone.

The coming transformation

Jesus' crucifixion shattered the hopes and dreams of his disciples. But on the third day, God's cruciform love triumphed over death, sin, and the devil. Jesus' resurrected and transformed body is a prototype of the transformation awaiting everyone and everything at the end of the age. As "the firstborn" (Colossians 1:18; Revelation 1:5) and "the firstfruits" (1 Corinthians 15:20–23) of the coming kingdom, the resurrected Christ embodies the hope of ultimate renewal.

This is why Jesus' appearance at the end of the age is central to the good news in the New Testament. Yes, Jesus and the authors of the New Testament warn believers to remain watchful and ready, for the end of the age appearance of Jesus will happen "in the twinkling of an eye" (1 Corinthians 15:52) and "like a thief in the night" (1 Thessalonians 5:2).[3] And yes, there are solemn reminders that the "Day of the Lord" will be a day of judgment which Paul likens to a fire that will burn away all that is incompatible with God's character and refine all that can be made compatible (1 Corinthians 3:12–15, compare Joel 2:31). Yet, the early church eagerly anticipated this day, for only through Christ's return could our broken world be healed.

Paul captures this hope when he encourages Christians to "live self-controlled, upright and godly lives in this present age, while we wait for the blessed hope—the appearing of the glory of our great God and Savior, Jesus Christ" (Titus 2:12–13). Similarly, he reminds the Philippians that "our citizenship is in heaven" and declares: "And we eagerly await a Savior from there, the Lord Jesus Christ, who, by the power that enables him to bring everything under his control, will transform our lowly bodies so they will be like his glorious body" (Philippians 3:20–21).

Our waiting is "eager" because only when Jesus appears will our "lowly" bodies be transformed into the likeness of his "glorious" resurrected body. No wonder the early Christians urgently prayed, *Maranatha*—Aramaic for "Come, Lord" (1 Corinthians 16:22).

Not only will our bodies be like his, but John proclaims, "When Christ appears, we shall be like him, for we shall see him as he is" (1 John 3:2). This reflects the ancient principle that like is known by like, discussed in chapter 4. In the end, we will finally know Jesus as he truly is because our character will be perfectly conformed to his. And it's not just humanity that longs for transformation. According to Paul, "the whole creation has been groaning as in the pains of childbirth right up to the present time" (Romans 8:22), yearning to be liberated from its "bondage to decay and brought into the freedom and glory of the children of God" (v. 21).

When God's kingdom is established on the "new earth," our present age's pain and sorrow will be replaced with unimaginable joy. Paul goes so far as to declare that "our present sufferings are not worth comparing with the glory that will be revealed in us" (Romans 8:18). Considering the nightmarish suffering so many endure in this life, Paul's statement suggests that the glory awaiting us is truly beyond comprehension.

He's coming soon!

One challenging aspect of the New Testament's perspective on Jesus' end times appearance is that, while we are repeatedly told that "no one knows the day or the hour" (Mark 13:32), it seems clear that both Jesus and the early Christians expected this to happen in their lifetimes.[4] This raises a challenging question: Were Jesus and the early Christians wrong?

N. T. Wright and a number of other New Testament scholars answer no. They argue that the apocalyptic language used by Jesus and the New Testament writers was common in Jewish thought, signifying "the end of the world as you know it" rather than the literal end of the world.[5] Indeed, this type of language was often used to describe significant historical events.[6] Most of these scholars agree that, in the case of Jesus and the early Christians, the end of the world "as they knew it" came with the destruction of the temple in 70 CE.

While I find this perspective helpful, I don't believe it fully resolves the tension. Even if the New Testament's apocalyptic imagery was partially fulfilled in 70 CE—when the Roman army destroyed Jerusalem, as well as the second temple—the ultimate transformation of creation that the early Christians anticipated—and that the whole creation groans for—obviously did not occur.

So, were Jesus and the New Testament writers mistaken? I would answer yes and no. Yes, they were factually mistaken in believing the final transformation of all things would occur in their lifetimes. But they were nevertheless right to live with this expectation because it reflects the mindset God wants his people to have. Why else would the New Testament so frequently emphasize the need for believers to be watchful and ready as they eagerly anticipate the Lord's return?

Having ignored this teaching for most of my life, I have been trying to adopt this mindset since I came to view this as one of the core messages of the New Testament several years ago. This switch has profoundly impacted my life.

For one thing, adopting this apocalyptic mindset has exposed idols I didn't know I had. For example, I always thought my academic research and writing were motivated purely by a desire to advance God's kingdom. But when I began anticipating Jesus' appearance at any moment, I've discovered that part of my motivation was tied to an idolatrous desire to create a respectable legacy. You don't worry about legacy if you're anticipating the Lord to appear at any moment. Letting go of this idol has been liberating.

Most importantly, living with the expectation that Jesus will soon appear has filled me with hope and peace. And at a time when it seems like the world is unraveling, this hope and peace couldn't be more precious.

A world in crisis

Throughout history, various groups of Christians have believed the end of the world was upon them based on their interpretation of Scripture.[7] Obviously, every one of them was mistaken. Rest assured; I'm not going to repeat their mistake. While we are called to live as though Jesus could return at any moment, we must also humbly acknowledge that this might not happen for another millennia or two or, who knows?

At the same time, it's hard to deny that we are living in a time of unprecedented peril. Many systemic scientists describe our predicament as a "polycrisis" or "metacrisis" because we are simultaneously facing a number of existential threats.[8] It is not without reason that anxiety and depression rates are rising sharply around the globe, especially among young people, as awareness of these threats grows.[9] On that note, if you are dealing with mental health issues, you should consider skipping ahead to the next section.

Here is a brief overview of the polycrisis we face.

For starters, social and political divides have significantly deepened over the last decade, fueled by cable news, the internet, and social media.[10] These tools have trapped many people in quarantined information bubbles, eroding shared trust in sources of information, in institutions and in social norms. As a result, democratic countries—which depend on these things—are struggling.[11] Most concerning, it is hard to see how this trend toward increasing social and political fragmentation and polarization can be reversed.

Meanwhile, the planet is warming at a breakneck pace.[12] The last ten years have been the hottest on record, with 2024 being the hottest yet. The Arctic has lost 95 percent of its ice since 1970 and our glaciers are melting at an alarming rate, putting millions of people at risk of water scarcity.[13] Our oceans are warming and becoming increasingly acidic, which is wreaking havoc with the oceanic ecosystem. Extreme weather events are becoming more frequent and more intense, as are forest fires. And in the coming decades we will likely be facing an enormous immigration crisis as entire regions of land become uninhabitable, whether because of scorching heat and famine or because of rising sea levels.[14] And most unfortunately, so long as we continue to pump ever-increasing amounts of carbon dioxide and other greenhouse gases into our atmosphere, weather chaos will almost certainly continue to intensify into the foreseeable future.

Simultaneously, we are witnessing an alarming loss of biodiversity. Species are going extinct at rates up to a thousand times faster than the natural baseline, driven by climate change, habitat destruction, and pollutants like microplastics and forever chemicals, which also threaten human fertility and health.[15] There have been at least five mass extinctions in earth's history, commonly defined as the rapid loss of 75 percent or more of all species on earth. A growing number of scientists suspect that we may now be experiencing a sixth mass extinction.[16]

On another front, humanity's reliance on finite oil reserves is increasingly precarious.[17] Most of the easily extracted oil has been used up, so companies need to drill deeper and resort to more extreme measures, such as fracking, to extract it. As extraction costs rise and reserves dwindle, the need to transition to renewable energy becomes ever more urgent. Yet, while green technology has made incredible advances over the last several years, it has so far only slightly slowed the rate at which our carbon dioxide emissions are accelerating because global energy demands are continually rising.

Which brings me to the underlying cause of these other existential threats. During the Industrial Revolution in the eighteenth and nineteenth centuries, the West adopted a perpetual growth economic model, which means our economy must continually grow, or it will implode. Since the end of World War II this has become the economic model for the entire globe. Unfortunately, this means that humans must consume more and more resources and produce more and more waste, when we are already consuming more and producing more waste than our earth can naturally process. The rapid degradation of our environment we are now experiencing is the result. In scientific terms, we have exceeded earth's "carrying capacity" and are in a state of "overshoot."[18] As MIT scientists demonstrated decades ago, there *are* limits to growth—and, as their "business as usual" model predicted, we are now running into them.[19]

However, it's not all bad news. Renewable energy sources such as solar, wind, and hydroelectric power are becoming increasingly affordable and widespread. According to the Environmental Performance Index (EPI), Denmark, the United Kingdom, Sweden, and a number of other countries have significantly lowered their carbon output and transitioned to renewable energy sources.[20] Additionally, while still in experimental stages and fraught with risks, emerging geoengineering technologies hold the potential to slow, and possibly eventually even reverse, the effects of global warming.

But so long as we—and this "we" is primarily all of us in the West who are the greatest beneficiaries of the world's perpetual growth narrative—are held captive to the ceaseless quest for more, our technological breakthroughs are only buying us time (and thank God for that). To live on a finite planet, we must honor its natural boundaries. In the end, it really is that simple.

Indigenous people have understood this and thus honor the earth and all that it brings forth.[21] Many of us in the West have forgotten this, and it may prove to be the greatest tragedy in history that the Europeans who conquered this land had no interest in learning anything from the people they were conquering. If ever there was a time for us to do so, it is now.

The people who should be first in line should be people who follow Jesus: all who know from Scripture that our Creator made humans responsible for the well-being of the earth and the environment (Genesis 1:26–28).

A kingdom response

We must do everything possible to reduce the damage we are currently doing to our shared biological home. And I believe we must do everything possible to buy us time to cut our greenhouse gas emissions and transition to clean energy. And, as I shared, there are some hopeful signs in technology as well.

But this is not where our ultimate hope is supposed to lie. As followers of Jesus, our ultimate hope is in the coming transformation and restoration of all things. And we are citizens of, and ambassadors of, an altogether unique kingdom. And so, to bring this book to a close, I'd like to briefly address what I believe is a distinctly kingdom way of responding to the polycrisis we currently face. What does faithfulness to the God who looks like Jesus look like in a world that is unraveling? I'll suggest four things.

First, and most importantly, if our world continues to unravel, as I suspect it will, it is imperative we hold fast to the blessed hope of Christ's reappearance and the "restoration of all things." We don't need to know when this will happen. Nor do we need to have clue what this will look like, because I don't believe we do. Jesus' first coming didn't look anything like the way people expected, and I see no reason to believe his second coming will be any less surprising. But when it seems to you that God has abandoned our world—as I confess it has sometimes seemed to me over the last several years—we must double down on the truth that Jesus is "God with us" (Matthew 1:23) and promised to never leave us or forsake us, *even unto "the end of the age"* (Matthew 28:20, emphasis added).

Moreover, the call to remain hopeful is not just for our sake, but for the sake of others. We cannot effectively help others as we head into an increasingly risky future, if we ourselves fall into despair. To the contrary, Scripture enjoins us to "be prepared to give an answer to everyone who asks you to give the reason for the hope that you have" (1 Peter 3:15).

The world is being afflicted with despair, and we've got the only antidote.

Second, I encourage Jesus followers to opt out of the perpetual growth narrative, and the perpetual growth economy, as much as possible, for this is the main driver of the polycrisis we are facing. This economic model reflects the same self-ascending and self-destructive mindset as Lucifer, when he imagined he could ignore the boundaries set by God and ascend to any height he could imagine (Isaiah 14:12–15). But he could only overshoot his God-given boundaries for so long. He fell, and he "destroyed [his] land and killed [his] people" in the process (v. 20).

The kingdom call is to resist this perpetual-ascent mindset by becoming content with what we have while practicing generosity to others who have less (Luke 14:33–34; Philippians 4:11–13). A first step might be to simply stop buying stuff you don't need and to avoid buying anything new if buying used will do.

Third, we must always remember that, regardless of our circumstances, we are called to love others the way God has loved us by become one of us (Ephesians 5:1–2). Far from hoping to be raptured out of our hurting world, imitating Jesus requires us to live in solidarity with it. Love doesn't abandon people in their pain—it moves toward them, as Christ moved toward us. If things continue to worsen, governments and institutions will likely struggle to meet growing needs, and the church will have an opportunity to display God's love by becoming this safety net for the hungry, the hurting, and the marginalized.

If we continue down the path we are currently heading, resources will become scarcer and many people will be inclined to hoard. Our call is to move in the opposite direction. Will we rise to the occasion?

Fourth, many of us live in a country that solicits our opinion every two years about who should serve in what governmental capacity. I knowing there are a multitude of issues that a person must consider when casting their vote, but I encourage kingdom people to place addressing global warming and the other existential threats we are currently facing at the top of your priority list.

Finally, we are God's designated stewards over his incredible earth. We are called to love and cherish the earth, which means we must be willing to minimize whatever negative impact our lifestyle is having on its well-being. And this means you have to find this out. So, I encourage those who haven't done so to embark on a learning journey. And in doing so, you'll find out the numerous little adjustments you can make in your day-to-day life that can lower your carbon footprint.[22]

You may be tempted to think that your lifestyle adjustments can't make any real difference. But as followers of Jesus, our motivation shouldn't be tethered to outcomes. Rather, it should be tethered to faithfulness. We should do all we can do to help the environment and animals, not only because it does make a difference, but most fundamentally because this is what fulfilling the Creator's first mandate to care for the earth and animal kingdom looks like (Genesis 1:26–28). This is what loving the earth and its ten million species of living creatures looks like.

Jesus reveals what God is truly like, and therefore what God has always been like. God had the other-oriented loving character he reveals in Jesus when he created the world. While it was often obscured by his people, God has had this same cruciform character as he worked through his people throughout history with the aim of blessing the whole world. And God will display this same cruciform character when he decides it's time to bring our current fallen age to a close.

If we remain resolute in our conviction that God looks like Jesus, we can trust that God will, in the end, do right by everyone. For, when all things are finally restored and God is all in all, it will be unimaginably glorious, for all of us and for everything, rendering the suffering of our present age insignificant (Romans 8:18).

In the uncertain and potentially frightful times in which we live, let us remain anchored in this blessed hope. Maranatha!

Appendix

My Approach to Scripture

There are three quick points to make about the approach to Scripture I assume in this work.

First, I adopt a canonical approach to Scripture. While I fully acknowledge the unique voice of each biblical author, I also affirm the divine authorship of the canon. This conviction allows me to interpret individual passages in light of the entire canon.[1]

Second, while I affirm the importance of understanding the original intent of the biblical authors, I also subscribe to the basic tenets of the Theological Interpretation of Scripture (TIS).[2] This academic movement critiques a strictly historical-critical approach to Scripture and advocates for reclaiming the church's traditional conviction that the Bible contains a surplus of meaning (*sensus plenior*). In other words, biblical passages can and do carry Spirit-inspired layers of meaning that transcend the original author's intent.

Third, though biblical criticism has its place in understanding Scripture, I also align with TIS in believing that reading Scripture as God's inspired story requires us to suspend critical concerns and approach the text with "innocent eyes"—what some call a "second naïveté." The goal is to read and hear Scripture as the earliest Christians did, before the advent of biblical criticism introduced endless questions that clouded this process.

Accordingly, when I speak of biblical characters and stories, I do so from within the narrative of Scripture, which I regard as divinely inspired. I am not attempting to weigh in on historical-critical questions about the historicity of these characters or events. Similarly, when I refer to the traditional authorship of a disputed canonical book (e.g., Ephesians, 2 Timothy), I do so for the sake of convenience and out of respect for tradition, not as a means of settling authorship debates.

Acknowledgments

To M. Scott Boren, thank you for laying the foundation for this book. Your skillful synthesis and creative editing of material I had previously written provided the groundwork on which this work was built.

Jon Hand, your relentless encouragement to me to write this book and to invite Scott to help jump-start the process have been invaluable. Thank you.

I am also profoundly thankful to the dedicated staff at Herald Press for making the publication process both seamless and enjoyable. Special thanks go to Elisabeth Ivey and Rachel Martens for their exceptional editorial expertise and keen attention to detail.

To Meghan Good, thank you for graciously agreeing to write the foreword to this book and for being a trusted friend over the past fifteen years. Your kindness and wisdom have meant so much to me.

As always, I am profoundly grateful for my beloved wife of forty-four years, Shelley Boyd. You are the anchor of my life, holding everything together—even when living with a husband whose ADHD leaves his brain scattered and lacking organization. I love you beyond measure.

Finally, this book would obviously not exist were it not for the God who looks like Jesus. Thank you for your unfathomable love—for me, for humanity, and for all creation. In a world that feels increasingly fragile, your eternal hope sustains us.

Notes

Introduction

1 Throughout this book, when I speak of our "mental image of God," I am referring to everything that a person experiences in their mind when they contemplate God. The most foundational task of discipleship is to cooperate with the Spirit to take all of our mental images of God "captive . . . to Christ" (2 Corinthians 10:5).

2 For readers who are interested in the key methodological convictions underpinning my approach to Scripture, see the appendix.

Chapter 1

1 "The Meaning of Life," Gay Byrne, February 1, 2015, on RTÉ One (Ireland's national public service broadcaster).

2 I prefer referring to Scripture as "the inspired story of God" rather than the more traditional "inspired word of God" because Jesus alone is the "Word of God" (John1:1, 14) and he shouldn't have any competition, and because the Bible is a story, not a word.

3 To deny that this depiction of Yahweh resembles Jesus is *not* to deny that this depiction is divinely inspired or that it has something to teach us. Indeed, in chapters 3 and 4 I will demonstrate how this depiction (and all violent biblical depictions of God) bear witness to the God who is supremely revealed in Jesus' self-sacrificial death on the cross.

4 See Richard Bauckham, "The Divinity of Jesus Christ in the Epistle to the Hebrews," in *The Epistle to the Hebrews and Christian Theology*, ed. Richard Bauckham, Daniel Driver, Trevor Hart, and Nathan MacDonald (Eerdmans, 2009), 15–36.

5 Michael Ramsey, *God, Christ and the World: A Study in Contemporary Theology* (SCM Press, 1969), 9.

6 On the gnostic background to this passage, see Harold A. Merklinger, "Pleroma and Christology," *Concordia Theological Monthly* 36, no. 1 (1965): 61–74.

7 Hans Urs von Balthasar, *Explorations in Theology*, vol. 1, *The Word Made Flesh*, trans. A. V. Littledale and Alexander Dru (Ignatius Press, 1989), 13.

8 Scott Swain, *Trinity, Revelation and Reading: A Theological Introduction to the Bible and Its Interpretation* (T&T Clark, 2011), 25; see also 37.

9 See Craig Koester, "Expressions of Double Meaning and Their Function in John," in *New Testament Studies* 31, no. 1 (January 1985): 96–112.

10 Derek Flood, *Disarming Scripture: Cherry-Picking Liberals, Violence-Loving Conservatives, and Why We All Need to Learn to Read the Bible Like Jesus Did* (Metanoia Books, 2014), 24.

11 Kenneth Sparks, *Sacred Word, Broken Word: Biblical Authority and the Dark Side of Scripture* (Eerdmans, 2012), 105.

12 M. E. Boring, "Matthew," in *New Interpreter's Bible*, ed. Leander Keck, 12 vols. (Abingdon, 1994–2004), 8:188.

13 Flood, *Disarming Scripture*, 25.

14 For full discussions, see Robert Bowman Jr. and J. Ed Komoszewski, *Putting Jesus in His Place: The Case for the Deity of Christ* (Kegel, 2007).

15 For a solid defense of this position, see Thomas Morris, *The Logic of God Incarnate (Cornell University Press, 1986).*

16 Though it is focused on Moltmann's Christology, a good introduction to kenotic Christology is Samuel Youngs, *The Way of the Kenotic Christ: The Christology of Jürgen Moltmann* (Cascade Books, 2019).

Chapter 2

1 Paul Copan, *Is God a Moral Monster? Making Sense of the Old Testament God* (Baker, 2011), 193.

2 Paul Copan and Matthew Flannagan, *Did God Really Command Genocide? Coming to Terms with the Justice of God* (Baker, 2014), 83.

3 I would like to make it clear that when I refer to "the cross" throughout this book, I am not referring to Jesus' death to the exclusion of everything or anything else Jesus did and taught. I'm referring to the cross as the throughline and culminating expression of everything else.

4 D. A. Carson, *The Difficult Doctrine of the Love of God* (Crossway, 2000).

5 Jürgen Moltmann, *The Crucified God: The Cross and the Criterion and Criticism of Christian Theology* (Fortress, 1993 [orig. German, 1973]), 114.

6   Martin Kähler, *The So-Called Historical Jesus and the Historical Biblical Christ*, trans. Carl Braaten (Fortress Press, 1964), 80.

7   Richard Bauckham, *Jesus and the God of Israel:* God Crucified *and Other Studies on the New Testament's Christology of Divine Identity* (Eerdmans, 2008), 47–48.

8   Colin Gunton, *A Brief Theology of Revelation* (T&T Clark, 1985),121.

9   N. T. Wright, *The Day the Revolution Began: Rediscovering the Meaning of Jesus' Crucifixion* (Harper One, 2016), 227.

10   Gordon Fee, *Paul's Letter to the Philippians* (Eerdmans, 1995), 217.

11   Other passages commonly identified as mini-gospels are Romans 1:1–4; 1:16–17; 3:21–26; 1 Corinthians 1:18–25; 15:3–5; 2 Corinthians 5:18–21; Philippians 2:6–11; Colossians 1:15–20. See Michael J. Gorman, *Cruciformity: Paul's Narrative Spirituality of the Cross* (Eerdmans, 2001); Michael J. Gorman, *Inhabiting the Cruciform God: Kenosis, Justification, and Theosis in Paul's Narrative Soteriology* (Eerdmans, 2009).

12   Graham Tomlin, *The Power of the Cross: Theology and the Death of Christ in Paul, Luther, and Pascal* (Paternoster Press, 1999), 99.

13   N. T. Wright, *What Saint Paul Really Said: Was Paul of Tarsus the Real Founder of Christianity?* (Eerdmans, 1997), 69.

14   Moltmann, *Crucified God*, 37. See also 211–19, 223–31, 249–52.

15   Westminster Confession of Faith," ch. 3, "Of God's Eternal Decree," accessed December 20, 2024, https://www.apuritansmind.com/westminster-standards/chapter-3.

16   Daniel L. Migliore, *The Power of God* (Westminster Press, 1983), 63–64.

17   Rob Bell, Mark Driscoll, Lauren Winner, Efrem Smith, Rick Warren, Erwin McManus, and Frederica Mathewes-Green, "Seven Big Questions: Seven Leaders on Where the Church Is Headed," *Relevant Magazine*, January/February 2007, http://web.archive.org/web/20071013102203/http://relevantmagazine.com/god_article.php?id=7418.

18   For several examples of a nonviolent interpretation of Revelation, see Richard Bauckham, *The Theology of the Book of Revelation* (Cambridge University Press, 1993); Sigve Tonstad, *Revelation* (Baker Academic, 2019); Mark Bredin: *Jesus, Revolutionary of Peace: A Nonviolent Christology in the Book of Revelation* (Paternoster, 2003).

19   Mitchell Reddish, *Revelation* (Smyth & Helwys, 2001), 22.

20   G. B. Caird, *The Revelation of Saint John* (Hendrickson, 1993), 75.

21   On the cosmic battle being a battle of truth vs. deception, see Tonstad, *Revelation*.

Chapter 3

1 For a comprehensive treatment of Scripture's violent portraits of God, see Gregory Boyd, *The Crucifixion of the Warrior God*, 2 vols. (Fortress, 2017); Gregory Boyd, *Cross Vision: How the Crucifixion of Jesus Makes Sense of the Old Testament's Violence* (Fortress, 2017).

2 See the references in Boyd, *Crucifixion*, vol. 1, 22–30.

3 Kenneth Sparks, *Sacred Word, Broken Word: Biblical Authority and the Dark Side of Scripture* (Eerdmans, 2012), 38.

4 J. H. Lynch, "The First Crusade: Some Theological and Historical Context," in *Must Christianity be Violent? Reflections on History, Practice and Theology*, eds. Kenneth R. Chase and Alan Jacobs (Brazos, 2003), 28.

5 See Robert Allen Warrior, "Canaanites, Cowboys, and Indians: Deliverance, Conquest, and Liberation Theology Today," in *Native and Christian: Indigenous Voices on Religious Identity in the United States and Canada*, ed. James Treat (Routledge, 1996), 93–104; L. N. Reveria-Pagán, "Violence of the Conquistadors and Prophetic Imagination," in *Must Christianity Be Violent?*, 40–45.

6 Graham Goldsworthy, *Gospel-Centered Hermeneutics: Foundations and Principles of Evangelical Biblical Interpretation* (IVP Academic, 2010), 252.

7 Vern Poythress, *God-Centered Bible Interpretation* (P&R Publishing), 60.

8 Goldsworthy, *Gospel-Centered Hermeneutics*, 252.

9 Hans Urs von Balthasar, *Mysterium Paschale: The Mystery of Easter*, trans. Aidan Nichols (T&T Clark, 1990), 15. On specific ways in which the Old Testament points toward the cross, see Balthasar, 15–16, 71–75. This thesis is fleshed out marvelously in N. T. Wright, *The Day the Revolution Began: Reconsidering the Meaning of Jesus' Crucifixion* (Harper One, 2016).

10 Henri de Lubac, *Scripture in the Tradition*, trans. Luke O'Neill (Herder & Herder, 1968), chs. 2–3, pp. 85–230.

11 I have chosen to refer to the Spirit as "she" for the following reasons: (1) It is important to emphasize that both females and males are equally made in God's image (Genesis 1:27). (2) While the Greek word for "Spirit" (*pneuma*) is neuter, allowing flexibility in pronoun usage, the Hebrew word (*ruach*) is feminine, supporting the use of a female pronoun. (3) There is early church precedent, especially among Syriac-speaking Christians, for referring to the Spirit in feminine terms (see, e.g., Aphrahat, *Demonstrations*, trans. Adam Becker, *Aphrahat and Judaism* [Brill, 2003]). (4) Relating to God as "mother" has been profoundly healing for me, and it grieves me that such avenues of healing are not available to those who conceive of God in exclusively masculine terms.

12 Calvin, *Institutes* I.18, quoted in Benjamin Warfield, *The Inspiration and Authority of the Bible*, ed. Samuel Craig (P&R Publishing, 1970 [1948]), 109.

13 Gleason Archer Jr., *New International Encyclopedia of Bible Difficulties* (Zondervan, 2001).

14 Gregory A. Boyd, *Inspired Imperfection: How the Bible's Problems Enhance Its Divine Authority* (Fortress Press, 2020).

Chapter 4

1 Origen, *On First Principles*, trans. G. W. Butterworth (Peter Smith, 1973), 4.2.9 (p. 427). For an extensive discussion of Origen's cross-centered hermeneutic, see Gregory Boyd, *Crucifixion of the Warrior God: Interpreting the Old Testament's Violent Portraits of God in Light of the Cross*, 2 vols. (Fortress Press, 2017), vol. 1, 419–61.

2 Origen, *On First Principles* 4.2.9 (Butterworth, 285, 287).

3 Origen, *De Principia* 247.23, cited in Thomas F. Torrance, *Divine Meaning: Studies in Patristic Hermeneutics* (T&T Clark, 1985), 360.

4 Origen, *On First Principles* 4.2.7 (Butterworth, 282–83).

5 Origen, *On First Principles* 2.2.8 (Butterworth, 284).

6 Origen, *On First Principles* 4.2.1 (Butterworth, 271).

7 On allegorical interpretation in the ancient world, see Boyd, *Crucifixion of the Warrior God*, vol. 1, 420–24.

8 See Matthew Ramage, *Dark Passages of the Bible: Engaging Scripture with Benedict XVI and Thomas Aquinas* (Catholic University of America Press, 2013), 13.

9 For a more comprehensive treatment, see Boyd, *Crucifixion of the Warrior God*, vol. 1, 277–333.

10 For an informative table of the "Most Disturbing Conquest Texts," see Phillip Jenkins, *Laying Down the Sword: Why We Can't Ignore the Bible's Violent Verses* (HarperOne, 2011), 36–39.

11 For a deeper dive and for references, see Boyd, *Crucifixion of the Warrior God*, vol. 1, 293–302.

12 Kenton Sparks, *Sacred Word, Broken Word: Biblical Authority and the Dark Side of the Bible* (Eerdmans, 2012), 38.

13 See, e.g., Paul Copan, *Is God a Moral Monster? Making Sense of the Old Testament God* (Baker Books, 2011), 90–91; David Lamb, *God Behaving Badly: Is the God of the Old Testament Angry, Sexist and Racist?* (IVP Books, 2011); Christopher Wright, *Walking in the Ways of the Ethical Authority of the Old Testament* (Apollos, 1996), 112.

14 See Leviticus 18:21 and Jeremiah 32:35 for references to Molek worship.

15 Copan, *Is God a Moral Monster?*, 171.

16 See 1 Samuel 15.

17 This is why my initial *Crucifixion* book grew into a two-volume, 1,440-page book!

18 Exodus 3:11–12, 4:10–13; 32:19–20, 29–30; Numbers 20:7–12.

19 Vernard Eller, *War and Peace: From Genesis to Revelation* (Wipf and Stock, 2003 [1981]), 59. I would only add that the Israelites' failure to understand this truth is one and the same as their failure to understand the truth that God is nonviolent—though we can discern the Spirit breaking through to reveal this truth throughout the Old Testament. See, e.g., Psalm 46:9; Proverbs 16:7; Isaiah 2:4; 11:6–9; Micah 4:3–4; Hosea 2:18; Zechariah 9:10; Malachi 2:10.

Chapter 5

1 For two excellent overviews, see N. T. Wright, *The Day the Revolution Began: Reconsidering the Meaning of Jesus's Crucifixion* (HarperOne, 2016); and Scott McKnight, *Kingdom Conspiracy: Returning to the Radical Mission of the Local Church* (Brazos, 2014).

2 The Upper Room is part of Communitas, an innovative church-planting organization that seeks to spread the gospel by addressing the practical needs of people. For information, visit GoCommunitas.org.

3 On this movement, see Meghan Good, *Divine Gravity: Sparking a Movement to Recover a Better Christian Story* (Herald Press, 2023). One organization that is becoming home for many Jesus-centered people who are rethinking what it means to be a "church" is the Jesus Collective (JesusCollective.com).

4 See David Kinnaman and Gabe Lyons, *unChristian: What a New Generation Really Thinks About Christianity . . . and Why It Matters* (Baker Books, 2007); Barna Group, *Churchless: Understanding Today's Unchurched and How to Connect with Them* (Tyndale Momentum, 2014).

5 Jacques Ellul, *The Subversion of Christianity*, trans. Geoffrey W. Bormiley (Eerdmans, 1986), 18. See also Gregory Boyd, *The Myth of a Christian Nation: How the Quest for Political Power Is Destroying the Church* (Zondervan, 2004).

6 E.g., John 13:34–35; Romans 12:10;15:7; Galatians 5:13; 6:2; Ephesians 4:2, 32; Colossians 3:13, 16; 1 Thessalonians 5:11.

Chapter 6

1 For a more in-depth treatment, see Gregory A. Boyd, *Crucifixion of the Warrior God: Interpreting the Old Testament's Violent Portraits of God in Light of the Cross*, 2 vols. (Fortress Press, 2017), vol. 2, 652–83. For a list of works that argue that the classical view of God is anchored in ancient Greek philosophy more than Scripture, see Boyd, *Crucifixion*, vol. 2, 1331–32.

2 Aquinas, *Summa Theologica*, trans. Fathers of the English Dominican Province (Benziger Brothers, 1947), Question 9, article 1, 88.

3 Aquinas, *Summa Theologica*, Question 13, article 7, 54.

4 Herbert McCabe, *God Matters* (Continuum, 1987), 46.

5 On the Greek philosophical background to the classical conception of God, see Clark Pinnock, *Most Moved Mover: A Theology of God's Openness* (Baker/Paternoster, 2001); Rem B. Edwards, "The Pagan Dogma of the Absolute Unchangeableness of God," *Religious Studies* 14 (1978): 305–13; and Harry A. Wolfson, *The Philosophy of the Church Fathers, Volume 1: Faith, Trinity, Incarnation* (Harvard University Press, 1956).

Chapter 7

1 For a critical overview, see Barbara Rossing, *The Rapture Exposed: The Message of Hope in the Book of Revelation* (Basic Books, 2004).

2 I find it helpful to remember that the NT speaks of Jesus' "return" in a wide variety of ways. For example, many passages speak of Jesus simply "appearing" (*phanaroo*; e.g., 2 Timothy 4:1, 8), or being "revealed" (*apokalypsis;* e.g., 1 Corinthians 1:7) at the end of the age. For an insightful discussion, see N. T. Wright, *Surprised by Hope: Rethinking Heaven, the Resurrection, and the Mission of the Church* (HarperOne, 2008), 123–36.

3 On warnings to be ready, see, e.g., Matthew 24:32–35, 43–51; 25:1–13; Luke 19:11–27; 1 Corinthians 16:13; 4:5–6; 1 Thessalonians 5:6–8; 1 Peter 4:7.

4 E.g., Matthew 10:33; 16:28; 24:34; 1 Corinthians 7:29–31; 1 Thessalonians 4:15–17; James 5: 8–9; 1 Peter 4:7.

5 See, e.g., Wright, *Surprised by Hope*; John J. Collins, *The Apocalyptic Imagination: An Introduction to the Jewish Matrix of Christianity*, 3rd edition (Eerdmans, 2016).

6 Isaiah 13:10; 34:4; Ezekiel 32:7–8; Joel 2:30–31; Acts 2:19–20.

7 Richard Kyle, *The Last Days Are Here Again: A History of the End Times* (Baker, 1998).

8 E.g., Michael Albert, *Navigating the Polycrisis: Mapping the Futures of Capitalism and the Earth* (MIT Press, 2024). A podcast that explores this "polycrisis" from a wide range of perspectives is *The Great Simplification*, hosted by Nate Hagen. For a good overview, see chapters 1–7 in Jem Bendell, *Breaking Together: A Freedom-Loving Response to Collapse* (Good Works, 2023).

9 See, e.g., Maria Ojala et. al. "Anxiety, Worry, and Grief in a Time of Environmental and Climate Crisis: A Narrative Review," *Annual Review of Environment and Resources* 46 (2021): 35–58; Ruby Harbour, "The Crisis of Youth Climate Anxiety," *The Ecologist*, September 14, 2021, https://theecologist.org/2021/sep/14/crisis-youth-climate-anxiety; Caroline Hickman et al., "Climate Anxiety in Children and Young People and Their Beliefs about Government Responses to Climate Change: A Global Survey," *The Lancet Planetary Health* 5, no. 12 (2021): 863–73.

10 E.g., Eli Pariser, *The Filter Bubble: How the New Personalized Web Is Changing What We Read and How We Think* (Penguin, 2011); Kathryn Brownell, *24/7 Politics: Cable Television and the Fragmenting of America from Watergate to Fox News* (Princeton University Press, 2024).

11 Examples of democratic countries that are currently experiencing instability or trending in a more authoritarian direction are the United States, Hungary, Venezuela, Mexico, India, Georgia, Poland, Brazil, Turkey, the Philippines, and South Korea.

12 Several of the information sources I rely on are Copernicus: Climate Change Service (Climate.Copernicus.eu); Climate.gov, hosted by the National Oceanic and Atmospheric Association (NOAA); and the work of climate scientist Paul Beckwith (PaulBeckwith.net). For a solid overview of the climate situation, see Bendell, *Breaking Together*, 175–208. For readers who may remain skeptical about global warming or that it is caused by human activity, I encourage you to visit SkepticalScience.com, which addresses arguments used by those who deny climate change.

13 Dahr Jamail, *The End of Ice: Bearing Witness and Finding Meaning in the Path of Climate Disruption* (New York: The New Press, 2019); Elizabeth Kolbert, *The Sixth Extinction: An Unnatural History* (Picador, 2014).

14 David Wallace-Wells, *The Uninhabitable Earth: Life After Warming* (Tim Duggan Books, 2019).

15 Shanna Swan with Stacey Coline, *Countdown: How Our Modern World Is Threatening Sperm Counts, Altering Male and Female Reproductive Development, and Imperiling the Future of the Human Race* (Scribner, 2020).

16 Kolbert, *Sixth Extinction*.

17 Listen to "Oil: It Was the Best of Fuels, It Was the Worst of Fuels," on *The Great Simplification* podcast, January 12, 2022.

18 The classic work on this is William R. Catton Jr., *Overshoot: The Ecological Basis of Revolutionary Change* (University of Illinois Press, 1980).

19 Donella Meadows, Dennis Meadows, Jørgen Randers, and William W. Behrens III, *The Limits to Growth: A Report for the Club of Rome's Project on the Predicament of Mankind* (Universe Books, 1972). Though these scholars were using a primitive computer and knew nothing about global warming, their predictions have proven remarkably prescient. See Gaya Herrington, "Update to Limits to Growth: Comparing the World3 Model with Empirical Data," *Journal of Industrial Ecology* 25, no. 3 (2021): 614–26.

20 America was ranked 43 out of 180.

21 See Robin Wall Kimmerer, *Braiding Sweetgrass: Indigenous Wisdom, Scientific Knowledge, and the Teachings of Plants* (Milkweed Editions, 2013).

22 A great podcast on this is *The Minimalists*, hosted by Joshua Fields Millburn and Ryan Nicodemus. For a list of other podcasts, see https://green.org/2023/05/09/top-ten-podcasts-about-sustainability.

Appendix

1 On the canonical approach, see Craig Bartholomew, Scott Hahn, Robin Parry, Christopher Seitz, and Al Wolters, eds., *Canon and Biblical Interpretation* (Zondervan, 2006).

2 On TIS, see Daniel J. Treier, *Introducing Theological Interpretation of Scripture* (Baker Academic, 2008).

The Authors

Gregory A. Boyd is an internationally recognized theologian, preacher, teacher, apologist, and author. He is the cofounder of Woodland Hills Church in Saint Paul, Minnesota, where he serves as senior pastor. Boyd has authored or coauthored numerous academic articles and nearly two dozen books, including his bestselling and award-winning *Letters from a Skeptic* and *Crucifixion of the Warrior God* as well as *Cross Vision*. He has been featured on the front page of the *New York Times* as well as on the *Charlie Rose Show*, CNN, National Public Radio, the BBC, and numerous other television and radio venues. Greg and his wife Shelley have been married for forty-four years. They have three children, six grandchildren, and an adorable but very eccentric dog. They live in Saint Paul, Minnesota.

M. Scott Boren is the founder of the Center for Community and Mission, a consulting and training ministry that helps churches develop effective small groups and equips leaders for missional church life. He is the author of numerous books, including *Missional Small Groups* and *Difference Makers: An Action Guide for Jesus Followers*. He previously served for six years as one of the pastors at Woodland Hills Church in Saint Paul, Minnesota. He holds a master's degree in New Testament studies from Regent College and a doctorate from Luther Seminary. He lives in the Twin Cities with his wife Shawna and their four children.

Jesus Collective

About Jesus Collective

God is at work raising up a movement of churches, ministries, and disciples all around the world that are passionate about advancing a Jesus-centered, Jesus-looking kingdom.

This is a movement with roots in the Radical Reformation that welcomes Jesus followers from a wide range of backgrounds, traditions, and contexts. We place Jesus at the center of everything, choosing in our differences to unite around Christ in our increasingly post-Christian and polarized world.

Jesus Collective exists to amplify this movement, providing resources and relationship for those who choose to participate in more hopeful Jesus-centered expressions of faith.

In partnership with Herald Press, we are pleased to offer a line of books to fuel the Jesus-centered movement and provide vision for a more hopeful and relevant vision of Jesus in this cultural moment.

Learn more at JesusCollective.com.